Do What the Spirit Says Do

☐ ☐ ☐

Do What the Spirit Says Do

An Oral History of the Civil Rights Struggle in Perry County, Alabama

Together for Hope Ministries, Cooperative Baptist Fellowship
and
Sowing Seeds of Hope

Susan M. Evans, Editor

Foreword by Robert M. Nash Jr.

Published by Together for Hope Press, Atlanta, GA

Copyright © 2012 Susan M. Evans
evsme1@gmail.com

All rights reserved.
ISBN-13: 978-1475183320

Cover design by Renee Lewin
Cover image: © R. Sampson/SXC.HU

Without limiting the rights under copyright reserved above, no portion of this publication may be reproduced, stored in or introduced into a retrieval system, or transmitted, in any form or by any means (electronic, mechanical, photocopying, recording, or otherwise), without the prior written permission of the copyright owner of this book.

The scanning, uploading, and distribution of this book via the Internet or via any other means without the permission of the publisher is illegal and punishable by law. Please purchase only authorized electronic editions and do not participate in or encourage electronic piracy of copyrightable materials. Your support of the editor's rights is appreciated.

This book is dedicated to the people of Perry County, particularly Marion and Uniontown, Alabama, whose stories inspire us all to faith and strengthen us to continue fighting for peace and justice between the races.

I'm gonna do what the Spirit says do
I'm gonna do what the Spirit says do

And what the Spirit says do, I'm gonna do, Lord, Lord
I'm gonna do what the Spirit says do

I'm gonna move when the Spirit says move . . .
I'm gonna pray when the Spirit says pray . . .
I'm gonna sing when the Spirit says sing . . .
I'm gonna fight when the Spirit says fight . . .

And what the Spirit says do, I'm gonna do, Lord, Lord
I'm gonna do what the Spirit says do

—An African-American spiritual

CONTENTS

	Foreword	i
	Preface	iii
	Acknowledgments	v
	Introduction	1
1	Mattie Mae Stephens Atkins	11
2	Walter Dobyne	43
3	Edward Daniel	63
4	Eleanor Drake	85
5	Reverend Richard Bryant	97
6	Evelyn Turner	129
7	Johnny Flowers	169

Foreword

As I read these oral histories of the civil rights struggle in Perry County, Alabama, I was reminded that nothing can match the power of stories. Stories draw attention to the experiences of a single person in the context of much larger historical, social and political forces and to the ways in which suffering and hope are intertwined in the midst of everyday life. These stories in particular remind me that life is a series of events, some of which we can control and some of which we cannot, and that most of what we can control are our own responses to what happens around us and to the impact that hatred and prejudice will have upon our own attitudes toward life and toward other human beings.

I lived in Marion, Alabama, for two years in the early 1990s while teaching on the faculty of Judson College. This experience was a formative one for me in which I came face-to-face with the very issues and tensions that these interviewees describe. I found myself living in the midst of paradox, both fighting a system of prejudice and discrimination and participating in that system as well. Such systems are complex, as these stories make plain. It is far easier to live with the injustice than it is to fight against it, no matter what the color of one's skin. Some people demand immediate change while others call for patience or, in many instances, prefer things to remain just as they are.

Some real heroes exist in these pages, whether among the interviewees themselves or within their stories. Few of these heroes ever intended to become heroes. Many were bystanders who found themselves thrust into prominent roles simply as a result of where they were at a given moment. Some paid the ultimate price with their lives. Others spoke a word of courage at just the moment that such a word was needed. Most simply wanted a better and more just life for themselves and for their children and grandchildren, and so they did what was necessary to create such a world.

In the movie *Shadowlands*, about the life of C. S. Lewis, a student of Lewis' tells him, "We read to know we're not alone." I have had a similar thought come to mind as I've read these stories that describe the challenges of oppression and the possibilities of hope in a rural county in the Black Belt of Alabama. These stories resonate so deeply because they are common human stories. They remind us that human beings are able to rise above the paralyzing realities of prejudice and injustice no matter where we live. They grab us somewhere deep down in our very souls, because we see ourselves in them, for good and for bad. And they remind us that we are not alone in our struggle, no matter how far we have to go on the journey toward that just world that we all so deeply crave.

Rob Nash
Cooperative Baptist Fellowship
Atlanta, GA
September 2011

Preface

This book project began as an attempt to collect the little-known stories of Perry County residents who hold powerful recollections of the civil rights movement during the 1950s and '60s. Originally conceived by Jeremy D. Lewis, formerly coordinator of Together for Hope Ministries in Atlanta, GA; Frances Ford, Executive Director of Sowing Seeds of Hope in Marion, AL; and Barbara Thompson, professional writer and president of Pathway Communications Group in Atlanta, GA, this venture was intended to result in an expansive oral history preservation project in Perry County. There were dreams of creating an oral history museum and teaching schoolchildren how to conceptualize and implement their own oral history projects as a way of honoring their elders.

In light of challenging economic times, however, and the difficulty securing funding toward that effort, those dreams were placed on hold and the smaller project of capturing at least some of the stories of remaining Movement participants took shape. The interviews in this volume were conducted, digitally recorded, and transcribed by Susan M. Evans from Candler School of Theology in Atlanta, GA, for the Cooperative Baptist Fellowship Together for Hope ministry as a capacity-building initiative. This short publication consisting of transcripts from interviews with seven Perry County residents is the result of those efforts.

The interviews contained in this volume represent a rich variety of experiences and perspectives on the civil rights movement in Perry County, Alabama. Every effort has been made to preserve the integrity of each interview so that the storyteller's own choice of words, diction, and tone comes through. The interview transcripts were only moderately edited for clarity and readability.

Acknowledgments

Many thanks go to Jeremy D. Lewis, Barbara Thompson, and Frances Ford, who initially inspired efforts to collect and preserve the histories of Perry County residents involved in the civil rights movement.

Deep gratitude goes to Jeremy Lewis for turning his vision of an oral history project into reality. His leadership, energy and commitment to the community helped drive this project. Thanks also for his faith in me, a novice oral historian. Special thanks also go to Robert M. Nash Jr., Global Missions Coordinator for the Cooperative Baptist Fellowship in Atlanta, GA, who has supported this project from the start.

Special thanks also to Frances Ford for her vision, for identifying a wonderfully prolific and diverse group of storytellers to participate in this project, and for her ongoing encouragement and support.

Much gratitude goes to Barbara Thompson, who encouraged, mentored, inspired, and advised me from start to finish. Her expertise as a professional writer was truly invaluable.

Special thanks also to Tom Prevost for his leadership following Jeremy Lewis' departure from Together for Hope. Thanks to Tom for his enthusiasm and unwavering support in turning this into a book project, and for his assistance in editing transcripts.

Many thanks also to Faye Suttle, who went way beyond the call of duty by driving out to participant homes to drop off transcripts, for chasing down release forms and for mailing documents back to Atlanta for our records.

And finally, thanks to the people of Perry County, Alabama, particularly Marion and Uniontown, who welcomed me—a stranger—into the community. Deep gratitude goes to our interviewees, Ms. Mattie Mae Stephens Atkins, Mr. Walter Dobyne, Mayor Edward Daniel, Ms. Eleanor Drake, Reverend Richard Bryant, Ms. Evelyn Turner, and Mr. Johnny Flowers, for their interest in the project and for their willingness to share their stories so freely. It is my sincere hope that through this work their voices are lifted up and the legacy of Perry County, Alabama, is in some way celebrated.

Introduction

Under the night sky and the pale glow of street lamps, black citizens of Marion made their way from Zion United Methodist Church toward Perry County Jail to pray with civil rights organizer James Orange who had been held there for the last several days. It was February 18, 1965. Another mass meeting had just ended and under the leadership of Albert Turner Sr., Marion resident and aide to Martin Luther King Jr., participants were going to protest Orange's unjust incarceration. State troopers had already gathered outside the church and along the streets where the county courthouse stood in plain view—white with majestic columns running two stories high. They had descended upon Marion armed with guns, tear gas, and billy clubs, ready for battle. Even ordinary white citizens had been deputized for the occasion, handed guns and given the right to shoot. Among them was thirty-two-year-old James B. Fowler of Geneva County, Alabama, who, four decades later, would defend his behavior by saying that he came that night to save lives, not take them.[1]

Many a mass meeting had taken place at Zion United Methodist before then without incident or interference from state troopers. But this time something was different. Tensions had been rising. Students at the all-black Lincoln Normal School had begun protesting racial oppression and segregation with lunch counter sit-ins at white-only establishments. Led by James Orange, they boldly marched into restrooms marked

1

"white only" and drank from their water fountains. Within a few days local police had had enough. James Orange was put in jail. The students were arrested, booked, boarded onto busses, and scattered to prison camps all over Perry, Bibb, and Dallas counties.

Until February 18, blacks in Marion and Uniontown had been reluctant to join the Movement. They were at the mercy of white bosses and plantation owners who could fire them at whim. But when the children were arrested, parents became angry and they, too, began to protest unjust voter registration practices. White pollsters gave blacks written tests which posed obscure questions about America's constitution as a requirement for registration—questions that, as Evelyn Turner, wife of Albert Turner Sr., recalls, "They didn't even know the answers to!" Blacks also could not register unless they owned land or were sponsored by another black person who did.

Protesters marched the streets of Marion around the iconic courthouse every day singing spirituals and hymns in vehement opposition to voter registration practices. Soon, local police became agitated by these displays of defiance. And blacks were no longer going to tolerate injustice. The two sides converged on the evening of February 18, 1965, in front of Zion United Methodist Church—blacks marching outside its doors and state troopers lining surrounding roads.

Suddenly the street lamps went black. In the darkness, state troopers swarmed about, beating people with billy clubs. Blacks ran through the streets and behind buildings, jumping into bushes and gullies for cover. Soon, anyone who was black was beaten, whether young or old, involved with the Movement or not. Mattie Mae Stephens Atkins, an interviewee in this volume of work, remembers the severe beating of Reverend Dobyne who knelt quietly to the ground in trained, nonviolent posture, his hands over his head to shield himself from merciless blows. Other witnesses recall the man who had not attended the mass meeting at all, but was walking home from work that night. He was beaten severely and left on the roadside for dead.

Introduction

Twenty-six-year-old Jimmy Lee Jackson, an ordained deacon who had attended the mass meeting, ran with his mother and eighty-two-year-old grandfather to Mack's Café behind the church. A struggle ensued between Jimmy Lee and two state troopers when they began beating his mother and grandfather inside the café. Moments later, shots were fired, piercing Jimmy Lee's abdomen at very close range. He died in a Selma hospital after eight days. Nearly five decades later, James B. Fowler would admit to being the shooter. He would plead guilty to the charge of misdemeanor second-degree manslaughter in August 2010, and at age seventy-seven, sentenced to six months in jail for the crime.[2]

Black citizens of Marion were shocked as news of Jimmy Lee's death became known. They met to discuss their next course of action, and Movement participants say it was Miss Lucy Foster, an elderly lady, who proposed marching with Jimmy Lee's body to Montgomery and leaving it at the capitol building for Governor George Wallace to see. Marion was too far away from Montgomery to begin the march there. Selma seemed a more appropriate starting point. After all, Martin Luther King Jr. and the SCLC had chosen Selma as the seat of voter rights activity in Alabama. Thus, plans for the marches from Selma to Montgomery took shape.

What was supposed to have been one march became three as nonviolent demonstrators met with the brute force of Alabama state troopers. Marion residents say that those on the front lines were primarily from Perry County. Children and adults alike were beaten with billy clubs. Tear gas blinded and sickened the crowd. Whites raged from the sidelines, screaming obscenities. State troopers violently drove the demonstrators all the way back to Selma and many marchers were wounded or hospitalized. It was Sunday, March 7, 1965, and the day would come to be known as "Bloody Sunday."

Images of this violent melee drew the attention of the national media and President Lyndon B. Johnson. A few days later, black and white ministers, nuns, and other supporters from around the country poured into Selma. One of those persons was Viola Liuzzo, a young, white homemaker who came down from Michigan to participate in the struggle. She was shot to death by the Ku Klux Klan on Highway 80 one dark night while transporting blacks from Montgomery, to Selma, and to Marion. Many Perry County residents now speak of her as a hero—another martyr for the Movement.

On March 9, 1965, a second attempt was made to cross into Montgomery, and state troopers again confronted the more than fifteen hundred demonstrators with the threat of violence. Without incident, the marchers turned back. Several days later, at the urging of Martin Luther King Jr. and the infamous KKK murder of Rev. James Reeb, a white supporter from Boston, President Johnson intervened. He ordered military protection for a peaceful march to Montgomery, and on March 25, 1965, Martin Luther King Jr., Albert Turner Sr., Andrew Young, and other civil rights leaders led demonstrators from Marion and other parts of the country into Montgomery and onto the steps of the state capitol, where King delivered a speech to a crowd of onlookers. Five months later, President Johnson signed the landmark Voting Rights Act of 1965 with King standing at his side. It was a final, decisive blow to the Jim Crow laws of old.

To what might one attribute the groundswell of activism that took place in the small town of Marion, located almost thirty miles west of Selma? After all, it is worth noting that the neighboring community of Uniontown, similarly segregated and politically disenfranchised, never experienced the spark of activism that Marion did.

For one, Selma and the Black Belt region, including Marion, was strategically chosen by the SCLC (Southern Christian Leadership Conference) as the place to spark demonstrations for voter registration rights. In fact, Martin Luther King Jr. and his aides were always very deliberate and strategic in choosing places to launch campaigns. In early 1965 it became apparent that while Georgia had registered over seventy thousand blacks to vote, Governor Wallace's Alabama

Introduction

had registered virtually none. After carefully researching the racial climate using scouts who tested and measured the potential for violent police resistance, the SCLC focused its sights on Selma and the Black Belt region, including Marion, as the place to galvanize residents into action.[3]

Another important point emerges from the stories of the people who lived in Marion at that time: Marion as a town was already prepared for the Movement by the time mass meetings began there in 1965 despite initial fears that many people had about getting involved. At least a decade earlier a small group of black men, including Albert Turner Sr., would meet regularly—secretly—at a place in the woods called the Sportsman's Club to discuss the many injustices facing black people. When the SCLC began to hold mass meetings in Marion early in 1965, many of the residents were primed and ready to participate.

Additionally, the all-black Lincoln Normal School had been flourishing for nearly one hundred years in Marion, profoundly influencing the culture of the town by cultivating within blacks the virtues of discipline, knowledge, and self-respect. Coretta Scott King, wife of Martin Luther King Jr., credited her experience at the Lincoln School as being one of the most important aspects of her preparation for a life of courageous activism with Martin.[4] Marion residents who attended Lincoln attest to its profound impact upon the town. Their stories tell of how the presence of Lincoln inspired within black residents a culture of pride, inner strength, and confidence, making it possible for them to attend college and become leaders both nationally and within in their communities. In a study conducted by Horace Mann Bond in the late 1960s on the sociological backgrounds of five hundred blacks in America holding PhDs, he found that a large number of them had family roots in Marion and ties to the Lincoln Normal School. He concluded that Lincoln was "the foremost black secondary school that this country had ever known."[5]

There are other accidents of history that are uniquely associated with Marion and the Lincoln Normal School. Coretta

Scott went on to graduate from Lincoln as valedictorian of her class and won a scholarship to study at the nearly all-white Antioch College in Ohio.[6] She and Martin Luther King Jr. were married at her parents' home in Marion on June 18, 1953.[7] Andrew Young, former civil rights activist, U.S. congressman, and U.S. ambassador to the United Nations, arrived in Marion in the 1950s following his first year at Hartford Seminary to pastor a small Congregational church for the summer.[8] There he met his wife and partner in activism and ministry of over forty years, Jean Childs Young, who so impressed him with her spiritual strength and intelligence, no doubt emboldened by her upbringing in Marion and her own family's legacy at the Lincoln Normal School.[9] Albert Turner Sr., civil rights activist and close aide to Martin Luther King Jr., was also raised in Marion and attended the Lincoln Normal School, along with his wife and partner in activism, Evelyn. He became the lead SCLC organizer in Alabama and then a powerful local politician. Many residents speak of him as a giant in the Movement—a fearless leader who gave his life for the advancement of black people.

And finally, as with many survivors of social movements around the world, participants in the civil rights struggle in Marion attest to the presence of a spirit that seemed to usher in the Movement and create a momentum that did not end even after the marches to Montgomery did. This "spirit" was evident in the formation of those important, though clandestine meetings at the Sportsman's Club in the 1950s. Even more profoundly, the "spirit" was resident in the presence of the all-black Lincoln Normal School. And the "spirit" manifested in the hearts and minds of the teenagers who fearlessly challenged Jim Crow, spurring their reluctant parents to stand up and do the same.

Given the dearth of a written historical record on Marion's involvement in the Movement relative to neighboring Selma, a people's history of the region's grassroots struggle for fair voter registration practices is an important contribution to civil rights history in the South. This collection of oral histories represents

Introduction

a small portion of those voices, rich in diversity and perspective. Collectively they illustrate the need for further study and celebration of this small town in the Black Belt region of Alabama.

Susan M. Evans
March 2012
Atlanta, GA

Notes

[1] Associated Press. "1965 Civil Rights Killing Case Ends With Guilty Plea: Ex-Ala trooper gets 6 months in death that led to 'Bloody Sunday' Selma March." Crime and Courts on MSNBC.com. Updated November 15, 2010. [http://www.msnbc.msn.com/id/40196577/ns/us_news-crime_and_courts/t/civil-rights-killing-case-ends-guilty-plea/]. Accessed October 2, 2011.

[2] "James Bonard Fowler Pleads Guilty To Manslaughter In Death that Sparked Selma March." Huffington Post. November 15, 2010. [http://www.huffingtonpost.com/2010/11/15/james-bonard-fowler-guilty-_n_783625.html]. Accessed October 7, 2011.

[3] Coretta Scott King, *My Life with Martin Luther King Jr.* Revised Edition (New York: Henry Holt and Company, 1993), 235.

[4] Ibid., 35.

[5] Dwight B. Cammeron, Julian Bond, University of Alabama Center for Public Television and Radio, *The Alabama Experience: Where Once We Stood*. In series, *Unforgettable Experiences* (Tuscaloosa: University of Alabama). Produced for television, Videorecording, 1989.

Horace Mann Bond, *Black American Scholars: A Study of Their Beginnings* (Detroit: Balamp Publishing, 1972), 97–98.

[6] King, 39–43.

[7] Ibid., 69

[8] Andrew Young, *A Way Out of No Way: The Spirited Memoirs of Andrew Young* (Nashville: Nelson Publishers, 1994), 34–36.

[9] Ibid., 35-36.

Mattie Mae Stephens Atkins

Mattie Mae Stephens Atkins, African-American female, was the first woman elected to the Perry County Board of Education in the 1970s. She discusses her life growing up in Perry County and her involvement with the civil rights movement, particularly her experience encouraging blacks to register to vote. She recalls with moving, vivid detail her experience at the Zion United Methodist Church mass meeting the night Jimmy Lee Jackson was shot and the difficult days following. Mrs. Atkins also discusses in detail local politics during the years preceding the election of Marion's first black public officials and describes the political challenges facing the region during the 1970s and '80s, leading up to the present.

□ □ □

Tell me about your growing-up experiences—you said you grew up outside of Marion.

Well, I grew up in Uniontown. I am the daughter of Reverend Lester and Allie Mills Stephens. I am the eleventh child of twelve. Momma had eight girls and four boys. And I'm the eleventh child. We growed up on our own place. Our great-great-granddaddy—he bought this property in 1839, I believe, so I was never on a plantation. And I'm just thankful for the blessing—it's been in the family for over 130 years I believe.

Do you know how your family came to own that property?

Well, according to what we did, some background check—he lived in Virginia, from Virginia to South Carolina, and I think from South Carolina to Mississippi. They always told us that he was from Mississippi, but we did background checks to see where he is from South Carolina. And he moved from somewhere down there, but I don't know where he moved . . . but anyway, in Alabama . . . and in Perry County. But, the story was told that his old Mastah had—it was during the time when it's end of war, and they used to give they servants the money to hide, so we heard that he gave him the money to hide, say he didn't stop walking until he walked on to Alabama! [laughter] His old Mastah to hide.

And then he just left?

He just left . . . and came on to Alabama. And he probably just bought this property back then. And another story was that his wife Classy was cleaning up the house of her old Mastah, and the chil'ren was playing in the attic. And they found this bag, and run and say, "Momma, look what we found! Look what we found!" And she took the bag and she had on this big apron dress—and she said, "You ain't find nothing!" [gestures shooing them away and laughs] But anyway, he bought the land. I know we been on free land there since eighteen-something.

So this was after the war, or before the war?

I think it was after the war. I guess we, when he bought it, a lot of pressure during the time, but that was in the book—in the zone—that this was eighteen-something.

In what book?

It's in the—the—we got a copy of the deeds from the courthouse, and it's giving the date and everything, with a sign when he bought it.

So he came here by himself.

They said his brother was with him, but we don't have no account of the brother. So my dad say they never saw the brother or look where he went.

But anyway, we grow up on the farm, and my momma and daddy raised all of us to be grown. I had one brother, he died when he was about seventeen, eighteen, he had tuberculosis, and one day he took pneumonia on top of that, and he passed away. When all eleven . . . she raised them all married and have children—all but one of them. And so, then, I went to school at home. We had a one-room . . . little bit probably larger than this [gesturing in the room]. But anyway, first, sixth, second, third, and fourth grades—sixth grade . . . was taught there.

So it was your mother who taught you.

No, it was my cousin. She had been to school somehow. Think she had been to Lincoln, but anyway. If you got to the ninth grade you was able to teach. Something like that. But anyway, she was my cousin. And she taught the room was full, and she would have a switch, and when we would get out of order she would pop you with that switch, and you're weren't gonna even tell it! Because if you took it home, you was gonna get another one!

We had to obey her. She had a big classroom. And I think we did well in that crowded condition. Then after sixth grade, I went to Uniontown to the elementary school. And from there to the high school across the road from there; they call it the Perry County Training School. And that's where I finished twelfth grade, over there.

And can you give me some idea of what years we're talking about?

Probably 1950–51. I think when I left home, the elementary school was on place there and I went to Uniontown Elementary. They went as far as the seventh grade over there. Then from eighth grade I then transferred over to the Perry County Training School, which now is named R. C. Hatch. They tore down that old school and built a new school. And I finished high school in 1955. I didn't go anywhere. All my other sisters, when they finished school they left and went out to the big city [laughs]. Momma and Poppa had got a little bit of old in 'em. Her health had start failing her, and his had been failing him all his life. I don't know how he did it—raised all twelve children and he suffered with asthma. Some days you didn't know whether he was gonna live or die. But he made it. God took care of him. And Momma was right by his side.

We had the farm, and like I said, I helped with the farm. And so I didn't leave home after school was out. I stayed at home about a year. And 1956 in May—no, 1956 in April, Easter Sunday, that's when I met my husband. And we courted until November the 18th, the day I got married. But on the record, the preacher said November 7th. I don't see how he made that big a mistake. So after I got married, I had five children by 1965, and that's when the Movement started, in 1965. And how I got involved with that, was my husband's niece, they had started meetings in our community, but we didn't know about it, but that's where they started. And later on, they moved their meetings to town—to Marion, and that's where they started.

I don't know what prompted them to start at the school with the children, but anyway, we had a man here, his name is James Orange, and he and Albert Turner Sr., now, I was told that they went out into the schools after they had had meetings in Marion at the old society hall, upstairs. Back then they had a little building that they called "society" where they had nickel and dime collection raised for the buried people. So Society Hall was setting on this side of the funeral home.

But anyway, they started there after left them out the home—they started out there in the Sportsman Club, and so they moved the meetings over here. But anyway, trying to get the grown people to march, but they couldn't get them. So they went to their school, and I guess he talked with the children that evening or something, but anyway, when they got there that morning, they got off the busses, and they went on uptown with James Orange and Albert Turner, and there was another guy—but I can't remember him—and they started marchin'.

Mattie Mae Stephens Atkins

And that afternoon when school was out, my husband's Niecey came up to the house, when we got through milking she came over to the house, and she say, "We marched today!" Now they didn't tell her granddaddy about it. He said, "March! What you marchin' for?"

"We marching for the right to vote! And we went everywhere! Where it said 'white only' we went in all those places." And said, "The 'white café,' we went to the white café, order sandwich, we went to the 'white' fountain, we drank the water, we went to the bathroom where it said 'white only' and went in the courthouse." And they let 'em. . . . We had quite a few places around there which said "colored" and "white"—"colored" and "white." She said they went to all them places. He said, "What did you do?" She said, "We marched for the right to vote." She said, "We going back tomorrow." He said, "Well, you go back tomorrow, they gonna put y'all in jail." I had no idea they were gonna put them in jail.

And sure enough, they went back, tried to march again—they let 'em march to the courthouse, and when they got up there then they marched 'em on the buses . . . made 'em get on the buses. And then took 'em down to the prisons, the prisons down there on 80. They carried three or four busloads, all the kids that was on the march. And put 'em in prison. And so we didn't know they was in prison 'til that afternoon, when his sisters came home.

He had sisters too, going to school at the time. And when they got there they said . . . she marched with them folks—with them civil rights folks over there, and they put her in jail. He said, "Put her in jail"? He said . . . no . . . "Put her in prison!" And so they're down there in the prison down there—at the camp down there—Camp Selma. And so you can't get 'em out tonight. You might be able to get 'em out tomorrow. So they didn't go that night to try to get 'em out. So they went the next day. I don't think she spent but one night in prison. And then after that, next day, the grown people started to march. And when they started marching, they loaded all them up on the buses, and sent some to Linden, some to Bibb County, to fill all the jails up. And the next day, we started marching. . . . That's when I started.

What prompted you to start marching?

Well, after the children had started, and they got 'em out of jail, then we visited the mass meeting. They would have mass meeting every night, where everybody would get together, and then he would talk about it, tell 'em what we needed to do. And, we needed to have a right to vote. Become citizens just like the white folks were citizens. See, we had went over there to have the right to register, and they wouldn't let 'em register.

'Cause I went up there to get registered. And you had to name the Constitution, you had to write the amendments, and give you long 8½ x 16 sheet, all those questions to answer, and I didn't know any of it—I would just put something down there. And this is the way it was done, so that's what brought on the marching. So, Albert says we gonna march round the courthouse seven times every day, and we gonna sing and we gonna shout, clap hands, and shout "Freedom! Freedom!" You know, stuff like that. And we sung, "Freedom, oh, Freedom, oh me." And "Now do what the Spirit say do" [singing] or "I ain't gonna let nobody turn me around"—those are the songs we sang every day. And marched. And we had done that for seven weeks, I guess. But anyway, on this particular day after we had marched, they came and they pulled James Orange out of the march, and, uh, they took him out and put him in jail. We didn't know what that was all about. . . . They took white mens out and put him in jail. So many was there, you know, you didn't know who all was there. And you didn't know who would take somebody out unless somebody else in front of them would tell you what they had got.

So, this particular day they was marching in Selma, too, and, uh, Albert had different people to come in and speak on different nights. And on this particular night, the Reverend T. C. Vivia, he was in Selma, and he spoke and spoke in Marion. He was one of the civil rights preachers that was working with Dr. King. And they was marching in Selma, too, and the word went out that they was gonna kill James Orange that night. But we didn't stop, we went on to the meeting. And, uh, Reverend Vivia, he came up—the church was packed—like everybody who had walked that day was in the church that night. And we had a good mass meeting. He spoke, and after he got through speaking, they decided that they had heard that him and Jim Clarks had got into it that day.

Who's Jim Clarks?

He's high sheriff of Selma. And, he had got into it, and he had hit Jim Clarks in the mouth, so he was running when he come up this-a-way. Try'na hide. But somewhere probably know where he was going. And they sent state troopers up there that night. Everywhere you look, there was state troopers.

Oh, so that's what brought the state troopers in.

Right, and they had said then they was gonna try to kill him. I guess the folks in Marion was gonna go and get James Orange. But after they got through preaching, and they got him out, after they saw so many state troopers was swarming the place. And they slipped him out the back door. I went to the funeral home. And then, Lee—Hampton Lee, slipped him on out up the road to Birmingham. Like he was going to pick up a body—and so he drove the ambulance and took him on out of town. So, he got saved—he didn't get hurt.

And after Albert came back in church, he said, "Now, we're gonna march tonight." And church packed full of peoples. He say, "We're gonna march a nonviolent march, and I want everyone in the back just turn around, and march out. And we're gonna come around and meet y'all." And, everything was going out so peaceful and so loving. Said, "We're gonna go up and march until they decide that they'll turn James Orange out of jail tonight. And we're gonna have to take all night." So I don't know what was wrong with us, but the folk just had that feeling when they got out there, and a lot of them had almost got out of the church. I was about three paces from the door, and, uh, the church had a partitioning between it at the back door. You go in on this side and come out that door. You couldn't just go right straight out the door. You had to go from one side to the other. And by that time, they said to put the lights out, out there.

No, before that, they marched out everybody. They got up near the post office—the jail on the other side of the post office. And then, Bill Lawson was the high sheriff. And he ordered them to stop—"Stop! Don't go no further!" So they all stopped, and Reverend James Dobyne kneeled down to pray. And when he kneeled down to pray, they put the lights out. And they hit him in the back of his head with a billy club. And that's when the fight broke out. And they beated people so bad—everywhere. [paused—shedding tears] They beat 'em going and coming. And they was trying to come in the church, and Willie Lester Martin—God bless him, he passed a couple of weeks ago—he was at the door. He had just got to the door. And he said, "They's coming!" And they start beatin' him at the door. And then a bunch of mens had got to the door and, uh, he ran back in the church—I don't know where he got that chair from—but he grabbed a chair, he broke it, and then he ran back out that door. And all you could hear is [imitates sounds of fighting] just fighting and stomping and beating.

But anyway, he said they was beating them to keep them from coming inside. And then I whirled around, and I turned I was gonna go out the back door because I thought somebody was coming in. And by that time Albert run in the church. He said, "You can't go out there." He said, "They fighting—you all get back! Get back—get back, so these folks can come in!" So everybody made room for them who was out there gettin' beat. [paused—crying] I'm sorry. [She takes a moment]

And, uh, he got back in church. And then, uh, I hadn't started gettin' out. I didn't know too many peoples that were there that night. I had five children. I hadn't started no getting out until this march start. And, uh, two old mens—one of 'em was my neighbor, that was Ben Norflick. They hit him in the head and put a big knot up here [gesturing]—right there—back of the head. And Lee Jones—he lived up the street and they hit him in the head, right up there—he had a big knot. But anyway, it was so sad that night, and everybody what could got back in the church. All them that couldn't, they run 'em down the hill, they jumped in gulleys. I was talking with this guy the other day—he said, "We jumped in that gulley—back of Piggly Wiggly." And I don't see how they didn't get cut up with glass and stuff. And he said where would a guy live, he called 'im "Points." He said, "Points ran down the railroad track. We told 'im, "No, Point's didn't," cause when we got up to Flurk house, we took Flurk home, call the place on the hill uptown there, he was up there—that's cause he walked up to the truck, and we was puttin' Flurk out, and he come out there to the car. He said, "The hell break out down there tonight!" And he had Dalston and Dalloway.

But anyway, it didn't stop there. They beat up folkses that wasn't even in the Movement. And, um, Mr. Lewis. He worked at M.I.,[1] and he was on his way home. And they pull him over, and beated him up, and left him side of the road, dead. He said he just stopped breathing—somebody felt him and he said, "Leave him there." He said, "He'll finish shooting him." And he said, "Naw, don't shoot 'im. Just leave him there; he dead." And they left 'im there for dead.

But, after Albert got everybody in church there, calmed everybody down cause it was a lot of hollerin', round bout eleven or twelve o'clock then, I reckon, or later . . . 'cause most

---

[1] Marion Institute

of the time, when we had a mass meeting, it was about 10 o'clock before we could get out. Then we went to the door and Bill Lawson Moody was standing at the door. And he told us, said, "Y'all get outta the front of this door! So, let these folks go home." And, uh, everyone just sittin' there, afraid to go out. So I think one girl, she named Lois Carr, she was the first. She got up, and she said, "I'm going home." And after Lois left out, I told my husband, I said, "Let's go." I thought he was behind me. Then I left and went on out. But, uh, they didn't bother me. I started to go in between them, but you can go down the step and you can go straight, so I turned round to the right side, and went out there and sit in the car 'til the rest of 'em came out. But we didn't stop after that—we were right back there the next night. Had our mass—we marched and everything the next day, just like we had been—took peoples up there we tried to get 'em to register—they still wouldn't register. Did the same thing.

You go up there and they ask you to pass a test. No—not yet. And every day we'll do something like that—take folks up there for 'em to get registered, and they give 'em a paper to fill out. And they register nobody. So, we came back out—no, that same night—I'm sorry—It was the next day when we heard that Jimmy had got shot. And they say he ran up as far as the post office after they shot him. He was down in the café. And they had already beat up his granddaddy. And, he was in the café, when he got there they was beatin' on his momma. And he tried to stop it, say don't beat on his momma. And that's the time the state trooper turned around and shot him in the stomach. And he fell at the post office. And they say he beat him up again. And took him out there to the hospital in Marion—they wouldn't even wait on him. They had to take him to Selma. So, we didn't hear that until the next day. But we still didn't stop. We continued to march, we continued—every day after that we continued to march, and we continued to try to get them to register us—you know—but they just didn't. So finally Albert put on a boycott. He said, "Well, we gonna boycott the town. If they don't register us, we gonna boycott. And don't nobody buy no groceries out the store—don't buy nothin'."

And we boycotted the town. And you talk about them people stuck together. Lot of 'em stuck together and not goin' in there to get nothin' outta some of them stores. And that's why we don't have nothin' in Marion now. [Laughter] They shut them stores down, they left and went somewhere else!

Where did you go for groceries?

This man I was telling you about that got hit—he had a grocery store. And then they organized another grocery store down there called the Perry County Grocery. That the name of that store? Perry County Grocery, I believe. Right down the street. And they would stock that store—people go there—and buy. And I think it just pushed other people to go to Greensboro. 'Cause they wasn't boycottin'—they went other places and bought groceries. And, they just closed up the grocery store, 'cause Piggly Wiggly right down the hill from here—it got closed up. But it was a lotta people here then, and those peoples on plantations . . . they stuck together. 'Cause, uh, Marion and everybody lost all their business. But we continued to march and continued. About a couple of weeks later Jimmy died, I think—I think he lived almost two weeks. And after he died . . . he got shot on the eighteenth, I believe. But anyway, they buried him the next week.

Anyway, after they buried Jimmy, we still had our mass meeting every night. But before they buried him, Miss Lucy Foster—she was an elderly lady—she said, "Mr. Turner, we need to take Jimmy's body down there and place it on the capitol. And let Wallace see what he has done. Kill an innocent man." And he said, "Ms. Foster, we can't take the body; it done deteriorated." We have to carry a casket down there. And that's how, after that—after they buried him, they had another meeting. They wanted to start walking from Marion. And Albert told 'em that would be too far for 'em to walk. And so he said, "Well, let us march from Selma." That's what brought the march to Selma. But anyway, it was coming up to the first Sunday in March. So about three or four hundred people left Marion. I didn't get a chance to get in that march, 'cause I had to stay at home.

Did your husband march?

No, he didn't march Sunday either. But I told 'im, "If you don't march, let me go march." "Well, who's gonna see after the baby?" Like Ms. Viola Liuzzo—she left her baby. My baby was three months old. He say, "You got to see about this baby." And they were dairy farmers and they had to milk cows and everything. So—

"They," meaning—

Him and his daddy. And, uh, so he didn't go. Person like this— if he's assigned a job to do, he likes to do it. He's superintendent of the schools—of the Sunday Schools—and he's gonna be there.

But anyway, they went on down—they had to march, 'cause when we got from Sunday school, they was marching. I turned the radio on, and Lord have mercy. You heard the hollerin' and the screamin' and the horses running—and I stood up and said, "Oh, my God! They beatin' them folks!" I stood at the radio, and I cried. And it was so sad—a supervisor that used to work with me in the courthouse, she said it was so horrible—that tear gas, the billy clubs, the whips, the horses. And, she have a beautiful story to tell, but she said she just can't tell it. It just bring back too much memories. And she was kind of on the stout side—she was heavy. And she said this was her little angel—she don't know where that little boy came from. She said that little boy caught her hand, and said, "Run, lady, run!" And he was right along there with her—and they had to run all the way back to Ebenezer Baptist Church. She said, "When I got to the church, I looked for the little boy, and I ain't seen the little boy." But, she has a beautiful story—I said to her, "Why don't you tell it?" She said, "I just can't stand to talk about it."

But anyway, after that, then Dr. King, he got up—that march, where we didn't stop marching at the courthouse. And the meetings stayed—we kept up—continued to have the meetings. And, after the big march when they got the state troopers, I mean, not the state troopers, the National Guard . . . then they got a permit to march. Dr. King got a permit for them to walk all the way from Selma to Montgomery. And if they was attacked, that was the only way.

There was a lot of 'em on the way?

Yeah, they said some of the Klansmen broke in some of their tents or something. But they got 'em out before they harmed anybody. And then that Saturday, they marched from Selma to Montgomery . . . all the way. And when they got to Selma, people from everywhere—they had thousands of folks—met up there somewhere. And Dr. King spoke in Montgomery. And after that, Viola Liuzzo got shot—that Saturday—on her way back to Selma, I believe. Her husband say he saw her. He say he was backing out, and she turned around right in the front of him, so they could go back and take a load of peoples back to Selma. And this black guy was in the car with her. Now, he went to that march, but, uh, they didn't get in the other march. That Sunday march—wasn't in there, but the final march when they climaxed in Montgomery, it was in that march, and that's where Viola Liuzzo, when they was talking about a woman had got shot with a black man, a white woman was in there with her? He said that woman turned around right there in the front of me—say I saw her—and say she turned around.

This was a woman who was in the car ahead of—

Uh-uh. A black man was with Viola Liuzzo. So that's the reason they shot her, 'cause she was haulin' people that—I guess she had helped take 'em from Selma to Montgomery, and she was gonna take 'em back to Selma, from Montgomery back to Selma. And that's where she got shot. They said the Klansmen drove upside her and shot in the car—and shot her in the head. And she, the black guy what was riding with them, said he was riding with them, he got out and he ran. And then he ran so far . . . they couldn't find him. 'Cause they would've killed him too.

So, whatever happened to him?

I heard Rose say she had gotten to see him and talk with him. I don't know whether he came to the march this year or not, but she said he was still alive.

I wonder where he went that night?

Well, there was plenty bushes along the road that he could hide in. And if he had a chance to get out of the car before they got back there to check her—he was gone. They wouldn't had to have a dog to find him, if he got away. And later on, President Johnson signed the bill. And then after signing the bill, I continued to haul peoples to the polls—to the courthouse and register. I don't know how many I didn't register. But one day I had an ugly experience.

[MA pauses to answers her phone]

Anyway, we continued to haul people, and they still didn't want to register people.

Even after President Johnson signed?

Mmm-hmmm—they're giving us a hard time. The federal government came in here and they registered three thousand or more peoples. And they registered those people. But we continued every year, every year, you know, to do a voter registration drive. Somebody in that community—I know that mood in there—they had the children, I had applications with me, I go through there and register them. I registered a lot of folks—it's just that, uh, I worked with the absentee boxes. And, uh, when I go find out, go knocking doors, if they're not registered then sign 'em up if they not gonna go to the poll. If they gonna be out of town, then I sign 'em up for 'em to vote. And, uh . . .

And so you were working at the courthouse as well, as an employee?

Not then—let me see—'71, I wasn't working at all then—when we first started. I was at home, raising my baby, and nursing my baby. And we worked in the fields. I had cotton, corn, peanuts, sweet potato, and stuff like that. We farmed. And my husband, he went into dairy farming with his dad. But, uh, 1971, then I start working—I started writing insurance. And I wrote insurance 'til 1977. Let me see. Nineteen seventy-three I had another baby. My other baby that I had in the Movement, he was eight years old. So he eight years, I think nine months over the other one. I had one in '73, and I had my aunt, and she took care of him so I went back to writing insurance. And 1977, I got pregnant again, but I didn't have nobody to nurse him, because I didn't have my mother-in-law, because she was under the weather—she wasn't able. And then I had to stop working for a while. And, uh, I finally got somebody big enough to see about him. My children had other children big enough to see about him, and after I went up to Greensboro first, then I went to Health Tex and I worked up there almost nine years.

And, uh, then I came back to the courthouse and got a job, and worked there fifteen years. Fifteen years and six months, I think, and then I retired.

I was telling you, we continued to register people to vote, and haul them that don't have a way to get out. And 1978, [thinking] uh, 1966—that was after 1965, and 1966 was the election. And we couldn't get none of the peoples here in the city to run for county commissioner. They was still afraid. And so Albert Turner came out there to the house and got Ike out the field— my husband call him "Ike." He said, "Ike, you been to the army you oughtn't be scared of runnin' for nothing. We need somebody to break this barrier and not be so scary, and run for county commissioner," He said, "I ain't scared, I'll run," he said. "I don't know what the job all about." But he said, "We will teach about what the job is all about." And he said, "I got Willie Lester Martin to run." So my husband got Willie Lester Martin to run—was the two guys that run for county commissioner first. And then we had Pat Davis—he lived in town—he ran for sheriff, and Lucy Foster ran for Board of Education, and Reverend Langford ran for Board of Education. And Rheese Nelson, I think, run for Board of Education. But anyway, we had—

What was the third name? [chatted for a moment about that]

Rheese Nelson. I guess they had three openings at that time, but all of 'em was in a runoff. And we didn't know nothin' about it. 'Cause when we counted up that night, Ike had won, you know, over the rest of 'em, so we thought. And so when we counted 'em up, the other guys had absentee, and you can see how they gave Ike two absentee. And it was three in the race. So he had to have as many of those two put together. He had to have 51 percent of the vote. And he had to have fifty and then one vote more, he would have won it. But anyway, he was in a runoff . . . people hadn't been taught 'bout no runoff, and they didn't go back to the polls a second time. You know, we had quite a few to go, but it wasn't enough to beat the other man. So, that's what happened to all of 'em that year.

And so the other man was a white man, obviously.

Yes, he was white.

So he was that close.

That close.

And people didn't understand.

They didn't understand—the election.

But anyway, that didn't stop us either. We kept on. . . . 1970—I think 1976, we had, uh, Mr. Williams. He ran for the Board of Education. And he won his position, and I think, uh, Mr. Walter Melton, he won his position. That was county-wide election.

What was his name? Walter?

Walter Melton—and after he won. But, Mr. Williams, he wasn't able to take his position. He died and they had to appoint Ray to his position. And he lives in Uniontown. And 1978 was our year.

Sounds like it. Is that also the year that the first black sheriff was elected?

Right. That year we elected the first black woman, which was me [smiles], on the Board of Education. We elected me—first black woman, first lady on the Board. First time a lady had ever ran for the Board. Mmm-hmm—in Marion. We elected Clementine Essie—the first tax collector. We elected Warren Kynard, tax assessor; Clementine Essie, tax collector; Sheriff Hood, the first black sheriff, and me as the first lady Board member—we had two county commissioners—John Ward and Willie Sullivan. There was two county commissioners—that year we took over the county commissioner, we had three blacks.

What about Johnny Flowers?

He come on down later. He wasn't the first of 'em. He came in and ran against John Ward. But he did a good job while he was there. I was try'na see if there was anyone else.

How long were you on the Board of Education?

Well, I served twelve years, but the first six years, I served six years the first term, and I was there when they appointed the first black superintendent, Earnest L. Palmer.

[*more brief chatting about Earnest L. Palmer*]

We appointed him in '79. 'Cause I went in early, because the man who was my position had died. And then after he died, that spot was open—they didn't have nobody to serve and after I was elected, they went on and put me on the ballot. Mr. Shoult stayed there for a while, but he didn't stay long. And so, Earnest Palmer was assistant superintendent in Demopolis in Greene County. And, we got him appointed here. And we had enough blacks on measure to appoint a black superintendent. And, after my time was up for the first six years, the other end of the county had got angry with me and said that we shouldn't have got the men out of the county. They wasn't gonna support me, so—we wasn't in no districts so, uh, Obie Scott—that was Coretta Scott's dad—he ran in '84 and he was elected. And he carried out a four-year term and, in '88, the county was in district, so I ran again. And I got back elected. And I served then. I got back like two times. I served twelve years straight, and then I was the president of the Board for twelve years.

You know, you get folks who are angry with you, 'cause you don't do certain things they say do. They really went towards Mae with me, but they knowed I support the superintendent 100 percent—so they decided to get me out in 2000. That was just a certain group, now—they did everything. But, we didn't stop there—every year I would haul people to the poll, help folks at the poll, then the rest continued to register. So I said I [inaudible] everything every year. And later on we got our president.

That must have been a gratifying experience.

Oh, you wanna talk about hollerin' and shoutin' that night! [Laughter]

Did you go to the inauguration?

Oooh! I wanted to go so bad, but it was too cold. I couldn't afford to go up there. 'Cause my husband had got sick, and he's diabetic, and it's been two years, hasn't it? I couldn't go, even if I had wanted to go. His niece was there. She went. She said she wasn't even cold, she said . . . there was so many people. She said she put so much clothes on. And her feet didn't get cold, and nothin' didn't get cold. Just had to buckle up that day. [This niece was the same one who attended Lincoln Normal School and went to jail during the Movement.]

But I say our voting wasn't in vain. The work I'm doing out there wasn't in vain. I saw so many people that we needed in office—you know. And it's just been a blessing.

I had one bad experience. I had picked up three ladies and brought 'em over here to register. And I was on my way back home. And I was travelling [Highway] 14. And I saw this car when it dropped off the hill behind me. And I said, "Oh . . . that car driving so fast!" And I kept on my speed, you know. And I kept looking and I said, "Oh, my goodness!" I said, "This person, whoever—gonna hit me in the back!" So, there wasn't no bluff on the side, and you can just run down—you know, just slide down. You didn't have the ditch or nothing, and I just whooped off on the side, and I stopped. And he pulled right in the front of me and whooped around, come round the front of me.

And what he said to me, I don't know. But I just sat there and my knees went to knockin'. And finally he turned around and went back north. I said maybe I wasn't the person they were looking for. That's the conclusion I come up with. [Laughs] But I had three old ladies in the car with me, and one I had to beg her to get in. But she never did go to the poll—I had to vote her absentee! [Laughs] So I said, that was one of the bad experiences I had—being frightened, you know. I didn't know what was gonna happen to me.

Do What the Spirit Says Do

Were you frightened throughout the Movement? Beyond the day you were in the church that you talked about when everyone was being beaten?

Mmm-mmm! I talk about that now! I tell my husband—we talk about it. I say, you know what? After they done beat them folks all night that night, and all this stuff happened, didn't like no fear came over us. Whatever Albert told us to do we went right back and did! [Laughs]

Why do you think you weren't afraid?

That's what I wonder about! Then I told him, I say it was just like the Spirit—it was just a—you know—flow, look like, going through! And I told him—I say, I guess it was the Spirit, 'cause we were singin' every day: [sings] *"Now do what the Spirit say do!"* And you know, we would sing that song every day. And I guess the motivation that Albert had, he would just pump you up. And, we would sing that song, Freedom, oh, Freedom! Before I be a slave! It just got in us, and I feel like we meant it! [Laughs] 'Cause we weren't afraid to get out there—we had to have meant what we was saying!

And after we saw through—Like I said, I come up . . . we never had a hard time. We never been without bread. If I had to have some meat, my dad would go out there and hunt and kill a 'possum. [Laughs] We ate possum—I ain't eat no 'coon! [Laughter] And we had rabbits and squirrels, now. . . . He would just go out there and shoot 'em and bring 'em back there and we'd skin 'em, and Momma cook 'em and cook some rice, and make some gravy, and put over the rice and. [Laughs]

But like I said, it just was the flow. Just that Spirit had got in there, and we sung all those freedom songs, and they talk about how some of 'em had been suffering. And, uh, I guess we just got into it. That's the only day I got scared, when they run me off that road. I was so scared they were gonna hit me in the back, so one mind say, *Take the side of the road.* And that's what I did. And I travel the road by myself now—every which a-way.

And that is the only time somebody tackle me. Lotta people be tackled, beated up, but I just say the Lord take care of me. Just keep the faith and pray and keep going. [Laughs]

That's quite a story. How did you keep your family safe? Your children?

Well, my mother-in-law—she would be at home, and she didn't get out much. So she was right there in the house—then she had these grandkids, Diane and Jackie—they would help see about my children. They was big girls. My son had gotten to be a big-sized boy—he was nine, I think. And my daughter, she was eight right there behind him, but they were still little. My mother-in-law, she was right there, too . . . and then Jackie, she was about thirteen, and she helps feed. If it hadn't been for that, I probably couldn't have stayed out there like I did.

Just talking about education a little bit. And I didn't know that you were the first black woman to be elected to the Board of Education. I really want to hear about what happened with the desegregation of schools, but before that, what was your connection to the Lincoln School?

I didn't go to Lincoln.

Did others in your family go to Lincoln?

I think my oldest sister went to Lincoln. She the only one, I believe, went to Lincoln, 'cause, see . . . we didn't have no transportation. And my daddy had a cousin over here lived in Marion, and I think she boarded over there with her—lived with her, 'cause we didn't have no transportation when my other sisters went to school in Uniontown. I had three more sisters that finished before I did. And then, my baby sister, she finished after I did. So, five of us finished school. My brother—my baby brother—he's so contrary [laughs], he was kind of very slow. I won't say slow—he was very slow. But, he got a chance to learn how to read a little bit. And write—but he can figure up his money! [Laughs]

He did what?

I say, he can learn how to figure out the money, but he can't read or write, you know, worth nothing. So he dropped out of school, I think, about the eighth grade. He helped my dad with the farm, 'cause my daddy was fairly sick. My two oldest brothers, they went to the army. My second-oldest brother, my daddy put him in the camp, I think. He said he was sixteen. He didn't want to work in the fields. And my dad say he told 'im, "Baby, you have to work in the field. I can't let you stay here, 'cause you end up in jail." And so he put him in the CC camp, and they went all over the state settin' out pine. That's how all these pines got set out. But then so much out of his check would be sent to my dad to help take care of the rest of the family. So, that's how we made it.

Did he ever come back to Marion?

Oh yeah—after that, he was drafted in the army, and he stayed in the army. He fought in World War II—both my brothers did. My oldest brother, he got hurt in Virginia—they was fittin' to go over, and he messed around and stepped on a plank somehow, and he broke his foot. So, he never did get a chance to go overseas. But, he still stayed in Virginia, and they had something up there for him to do. So, my second-oldest brother, he fought in World War II, and anyway, he came home safe and didn't get hurt.

When you were registering people to vote—did you encounter any resistance from the people?

Well, a lot of 'em didn't want to go and I just had to talk 'em into going. [Laughs]

Why didn't people want to go?

They didn't know what it was all about. You know, back then, they didn't know what it was all about—what it meant or anything. So, like I said, those three old ladies—one of 'em sure didn't want to go. Lord, I can't think of her name right now. I just had to beg her. Think she had married a Green, but she wasn't a Green.

And the other was a Coast and they lived there right together. I said, "Mae, look she goin', now you come on, now! This is to help us out, so we can get the right folks in office. C'mon register for us!" And she come on. [Laughs] But I didn't have no problem with Albert getting the vote.

At the time you hadn't heard about it that much about registering to vote. 'Cause first time I remember was—I don't know exactly what year, I think it was after '55, prob'ly '56—I know I was at home, I was out of school, 'cause I graduated in '55. Might've been the week of '55 that my daddy got registered. And Jim Folsom—he was running for governor. Big Jim—they call him Big Jim Folsom. He was runnin' for governor. And my daddy went up and he got registered. And he got back and told Momma he had got registered to vote. And I said, "Registered to vote? What is that?" I didn't know. [Laughs] And he said, "Baby, when you get old enough, you get registered—become a citizen of the United States. And you can vote for president and governors and all." He said, "This year I have a chance to vote for the government."

And so you just were interested? That sparked your interest at that point?

That sparked me then. 'Cause then he went to talking about it—you know, telling me really what it meant. And he told Momma he got registered, and I think two or three others got registered that day.

How was he able to get registered?

My daddy was old—he was up in his sixties, 'cause he died in '65—yeah, he died in August of '65.

Oh wow. But, how did he overcome the resistance? How did he overcome in order to vote? Did someone help him?

Back then, they had this thing going—if you owned some land, or something like that—we had two hundred and fifty on the book. That saying they was registered. They said if you had some land, then you were qualified to register to vote. They had every—all kind of obstacles in our way, didn't we? That's sad. You know, I can see all the things they done to us, and I say, I wonder—how do they feel? How do they feel?

How do you think they might feel?

Really, I say they don't have no heart. They don't have no conscience. If you have a conscience you can feel something. But if you ain't got no conscience, you ain't gonna feel nothin'. 'Cause I don't know what happened at that council meeting in Selma. But I heard them talking, and say they didn't treat Viola Liuzzo's daughter right. And they're saying that the Mayor need to go out public on the air and beg apology. Now what happened down there, I really don't know. Somebody—says she was talking, and I don't know what happened. But they talked about that. You know, they had it yesterday on the radio.

Did the mayor ever do anything? Or, did anyone ever do anything about her death? About Viola Liuzzo's death?

Nothing. SCLC had put a marker down there at the spot. It's a really nice marker down there. On 80.

It's sitting up on a little hill and it got a marker in there and then it got a fence around it. Not too far from a church down there.

[*Brief conversation about where the marker is*]

It's on the right side.

Is it closer to Selma or Montgomery?

It's closer to Montgomery, you have to go to ——it's in Lowndes County. But it's right side of the road. As you going up hills, you go lookin' to your right. It's not too far from a little white church. [Long pause] We have had so much around here in Perry County. Just so much—trying to keep us from voting. You know, tried to keep Albert and Evelyn in prison and Spencer Hogue—they set Albert's house afire.

I had a chance to interview her as well, so she told me—we talked for three hours. She had a lot to say!

I know she did 'cause she was in—I just don't see how she took it—Albert gone every night! Every night. People just don't realize how that man gave his life up for us. He had a family, he took care of getting some food and some money—clothes, "Evelyn, what you want . . ." But he gone somewhere all the time. But you know, just like a father, being there with his family, he wasn't there. And little Albert doing the same thing. Out trying to make it better for us, and we don't appreciate it. I don't know what it gonna take for us to realize how peoples give their time trying to help us.

I think it takes listening to stories like yours and Ms. Turner's.

You think?

I do, because just listening to you is painting a picture in my mind of what it must have been like. And you know, now? When an election comes around? And I'm not going out there to vote? I'm going to think of what you told me!

And we got to go teaching our young people because this election coming up here—it's going to be a big election.

Oh, it's gonna be huge! Huge. The presidential election, right? And, you know, the recent Senate elections and Congress.

We just drove our feet—but I couldn't work like I usually work during this past election. I don't know what happened to me. I had fell, and pulled these muscles in here [gestures] and I didn't stop working, though. I didn't get up the absentees that I usually get up. I think I got around about forty. I usually get about eight or ninety—something like that. But I wasn't able to do it—I had a muscle pulled, and I had to walk holding my side! But I continued to work at the poll. And look like if I don't be there, and help them folks with theirs, they gonna vote the wrong way, 'cause they look for me—"Mattie, which a-way I's goin'?" Some of 'em say, "C'mon help me—I wanna be right!" [laughter]

Well, that's good at least people are asking you.

Yeah, they ask me—they look for me. If I ain't there, "Where Mattie?"

So you keep up with what's going on, on the national level also?

I kinda try to keep up with the national level, but not like I do my own community. But I know Obama is having a hard time

[*Conversation ensues about the 2012 presidential election and then a change of subject*]

I know Coretta Scott King spent her early years in the area.

Her house is right up the road. She was born here.

North Perry. She was born in North Perry. She went to school—elementary, there. Then she finished at Lincoln and then from there on she went to college. Yes, she born right up the road, there. About fifteen miles. I'm fifteen miles from here too.

Okay. Did you know her?

Uh-huh! But I learned her after, you know, the Movement started. I didn't know her before then, because I didn't go to school with her in Marion.

And now I didn't know her father, Obie Scott, got into politics as well, but you said that wasn't until the eighties, right?

Mattie Mae Stephens Atkins

Eighties. I think, '84. Let me see, I got elected in '78, '79, '80—'84, 'cause I did six years. The first board member did six years, then after that he did four years because, uh, '88 we had another election. He wasn't in my district. I was in district one. And he's another district and he didn't run no more. He's in a white district. So he didn't run anymore.

It was three peoples running, think there was Vann, Obie Scott, and myself. And Albert, he was smart—he said, "Mattie, we're gonna wipe our hand already, put in for districts." He said, "If the district line don't be approved when the election comes, I want you to go out there and pull out the next day." He said, "'Cause, I don't want you to get out there and try to run." 'Cause the peoples in Uniontown, they had already told me they wasn't gonna support me. I probably will end up in a runoff with Mr. Vann—the white guy." And he said, "I don't want that to happen." 'Cause they will go and support Mr. Vann—that's what he felt that way about it—in the runoff election. He said, "Just wait. When the last day of the line had been approved, then you have to take out, and we're gonna have to support Obie Scott." So that's how he got elected.

We know Uniontown was gonna support him. But I would've probably ended up in a runoff with Mr. Vann.

Why would they have supported Obie Scott over you?

Like I told you, the first black superintendent, they wanted to support Mr. Carr in Uniontown, but we just felt like he wasn't qualified enough. And after they fired Mr. Palmer, and then they got Mr. Carr. And then after they got Mr. Carr, I think, was in office for two years, and the State took over. Mr. Palmer, we was just—he was so smart, and he told them, he said, we need to close some schools. And he said, but don't close these schools——you're gonna go some $350,000 in the red. They said, "well, can't you get a loophole" He said, "All the loopholes been filled—I can't fill no more loopholes."

And so, my time ran out before his did. But after that they fired him—they wouldn't keep him no longer and they hired Mr. Carr. And the same thing Mr. Carr went in the red, just like—see he had hired a lot of teachers, but they was on grant program—had people write grants. And he said, "My grant writers, the grant money's gone, and we're gonna have to, you know, get rid of these teachers." They didn't want to do that—they said, "Let's go through the loophole." He said, "I can't go through no loophole." So they fired him. And then they hired Mr. Carr. And Mr. Carr wasn't here two years. Was he there two years? Well, I don't know.

Anyway, to keep on trying to hold those teachers, that's like they wanted to do. They didn't terminate the teachers, they didn't close the school. He went into three hundred and fifty thousand dollars red. The state came over and took over, used Mr. Palmer's plan, what he had told 'em. Closed the two schools . . .

So they came in and did what he wanted to do—

—what he wanted to do. The state did exactly—they took Mr. Palmer's plan, terminated all those teachers, and closed them schools just like he told them he had to do. Sure did. Obie Scott said, "What y'all say?" He would sleep a lot in the class—on the board—he'd sleep—he'd just raise up and [M.A. imitates sleeping sitting up in meetings]. But anyway, that's what happened there. We have had some struggles over the school system. Integration, and—they burned down East Perry School—but to bring it down. I was serving on another committee—what they call that committee? Three blacks, four blacks . . . think it's a biracial committee. And I was on there and had another man named Danburg. He would never vote for nothing. He always wanna handle—so we wanted to close East Perry School, they burned it down. And then, they wanted to build a new school in Hieberger and bring all these children from East Perry up there. So, they wouldn't vote with us, and we wouldn't vote with them. So they had to build East Perry back.

I'm amazed by all the political accomplishments that have taken place there.

Now we in control. [pauses to answer phone]

Well, they closed out Lincoln, and we had to fight our way to go to Frances [Frances Marion] built by the county—Perry County Board of Education, then after they finished the school, they closed down Lincoln, they extended the city limit out and they took the school.

They said it was a city school. And all the children had to be bussed to Uniontown. Children from East Perry had to be bussed to Uniontown. And they didn't want no blacks to go out there. Only a few blacks went out there when they first opened it up.

They didn't want any blacks to go to Uniontown?

No, Frances—'cause they extended it, and they took over as a city school. Nothing was going there but whites.

But then the whites ended up leaving the schools, isn't that right?

Oh yeah, but at the time they had a white superintendent in the city, and finally they had to let blacks come in there too. And then after we got more blacks in there than white, then they went to pulling theirs out. They didn't want to integrate with us, and finally had to close Westside, and we're talking about closing Hatch now. So this year, Hatch will be closed—we might not have [but] one for the whole county.

Really? That's gonna be a big school!

Yes it is. Pretty big, but we don't have the children like we used to have. Ladies not having babies like they used to. [laughs] You can look at your kindergarten and know what your school's gonna be like. They're decreasing—I don't see where they increasing. I haven't heard Mr. Hurd say anything about it lately, but anyway, they're talking about closing Hatch, I know that. And have one central high school and two elementary.

Getting back to the sixties for a moment, one thing I'm interested in is, I was asking about the voting and what it was like to encourage people to vote—you were telling me about that—would you say that there was real cohesiveness within the black community during that time, across generations, across ages?

Unity? Well, in the sixties when we started, we were united—we were together. Nineteen sixty-six, it was so many people's turn—we voted, over three thousand people. And after that, they started moving.

Moving physically away?

Physically moving—they left Perry County—a whole lot of them left Perry County. Some of 'em packed their clothes, and went to the polls, vote, and kept going! [Laughs] 'Cause the plantation owners had told them if they vote, they're gonna be put off the plain—and a lot of 'em just left—didn't give 'em time to tell them to go. They just left.

Where did people go?

They went to Fort Wayne, Chicago, Detroit—they really left. A lot of people left in the sixties. Sure did.

Oh, I didn't realize that. So it was really a huge number of people.

That's what they say—a huge number of people left. But we still had quite a few here. 'Cause some of 'em just get fed up. A lot of 'em still stayed on the plantation, a lot of 'em didn't. And they just found other places to move. And a lot of 'em moved to town. And moved here in these houses that was vacant. But we've been having good elections coming up. The sheriff—they turned out good. And came up to the president—I don't know where they come from. Peoples came to the poll out there. I had never seen—especially men. We had more mens to vote in this election—this last election for the president. Like I said, I don't know where they came from.

I think that was the case all over the country—people were just coming out of the woodwork.

They really did. Mens out there I had never seen. I said, "Where did these mens . . . ? I've been working at the polls all these—?" I said, "I never saw these faces before!"

But, we had a togetherness, you know, certain peoples you want to see put in office, they worked hard to get in there. Like, we elected our first black judge this past election. Mmm-hmm. She's a woman. She controls the courthouse—every office in there, but one. And then the district attorney. We could have had them if the folks in Uniontown knew how to act right. They did. We got every office in there, but one. And that's the district attorney.

Well, the last thing I want to ask about, actually, is I've heard some interesting stories about the relationship between Marion and Uniontown. Can you speak to that at all?

Well—I would say it like this. Mr. Hayden, he was the first mayor of Uniontown. He played a great part in controlling that part of the town. Albert Turner, he just was a citizen. And he played a great part in controlling this end of the town. During the sixties, Mayor Hayden never did invite Dr. King down there. 'Cause the head white guy had all the land and property. So he said if King had come down there, the streets of Uniontown would run down in blood, or something. But he never did invite him down there during the Movement. And they really didn't take part in it. Only a few, now, I hear Johnny Flowers said he was on the bridge. He was on the bridge, and I think he marched the fifty miles, I believe. That's what he said.

It was him, and I think, three more men—two more with him, I believe. It was three or four, he said, was on the bridge with him that Sunday. And he went, I believe he say, but like I heard him saying, he walked the whole fifty miles.

Yeah, he did tell me that.

After that, him and Albert got together, and they got to be friends, after he got elected. But, that's what really happened. So before we got anybody elected, I think we elected—finally elected Rheese Nelson, and uh, we walked to Melton, I believe.

Anyway, we didn't want to support Rheese. Really didn't want to support him. He's an Uncle Tom. I get along with him now pretty good. So, Ms. Childs and I and Albert got together, and she told Albert and said, "Until your two ends get together, we'll never get anybody elected." So Albert decided he'd get with Mr. Hayden, and the people said, "Mr. Hayden, come out with this ballot"—a sample ballot—it was yellow in 1978. And they got together. And that's how we elected all those folks. All those five or six people we elected was in 1978. So we were together.

So you had to come together in order to elect all those—

Right. For fear was running kind of wide. Now we're in the district. And the district controls who we put in office now. They listen at the leaders. Some do and some don't. But with the good leaders, the followers get out there and work hard enough. They almost overcome the other people that don't want to be with us. So, I'm one of them, I got another friend, Ms. Adery—Willie Mae Adery. She works at the Board of Registrar at the courthouse.

And if we had a grant, we would interview all these people that we're mentioning.

Well, I think that about covers it.

Walter Dobyne

Walter Dobyne, an African-American male, sixty-four years old, speaks about his life growing up on the Sprott plantation located just outside of Marion. He discusses in detail his experience as a young Lincoln student involved with sit-ins and mass meetings in Marion, and his participation in the marches from Selma to Montgomery. He gives an especially vivid account of his experience on "Bloody Sunday."

□ □ □

When were you born?

August the 10th, '47.

And you've lived in Marion most of your life?

Yes, really, outside of Marion—I was born in Sprott, Alabama, which is about seven miles out of Marion, in one of the neighborhoods around Marion. Sprott, Alabama. And I think about '62, we moved over to Marion city limit—within the city limits of Marion. And I did go to Lincoln High School.

How many brothers and sisters do you have?

Five brothers and three sisters.

And did all of you go to Lincoln?

No, the oldest three went to Lincoln, 'cause the year the civil rights movement started, they closed Lincoln down the next year. Lincoln High School used to be a college. A high school and college together, Julian Bond did a film on Lincoln High

School and the history of Lincoln High School.

Were you involved with [the Movement]?

Yeah. Dr. King was in Marion and we decided that we were gonna have a sit-in in Marion, in all the white-only establishments. And so that called for Lincoln High School to march off-campus and march downtown on the day the civil rights movement started in Marion. And me and Martha Dixon led the students off-campus because the sit-in and everything—all was handled, and the sit-in and everything was performed by students. There wasn't no adults or nothin' involved in the beginning of the civil rights movement.

It was just students, and students marched from Lincoln, downtown to the church and from there, they set up groups to go and have sit-ins in establishments in Marion, and I went into Marion Drugs—a drugstore with a little bar in it, you know, a malt shop and stuff—you know, it was like the good old days on television. We went in—the four of us went in and sit in the drugstore. And they served us Coke with salt in it.

And—we sat around for a while after they put salt in the drink . . . and when we left, I carried one of the Cokes out to Zion United Methodist Church, and the white women—they turned just as red when I picked that Coke glass up and carried it out of the drugstore. And we sat in at all the cafés, and everything around in Marion, and by 12 o'clock they rounded all of us up and locked the door. And the fence around the jail . . .

Do you remember where you were put in jail?

Selma—prison camp. Selma. They carried the whole school down there and locked us up in the prison camp. Some of us stayed down there up to two days. Until the parents got us out. I was there overnight. A parent had to come down and sign for us to get out—sign a bond.

And what were those conditions like?

Just a barb-wire fence. It was in the regular prison camp. And they had us out in the fenced-in area, in the prison camp down there.

So you slept outside?

Yeah. They weren't equipped to handle that many students. They had to take the school bus and bus us down to the prison camp. And, that night, about 8 or 9 o'clock, they finally got around to feeding us. Cornbread and lima beans. Big ol' round lima beans and cornbread. Everyday.

The prison camp—they didn't show no hostility or nothing, 'cause they just locked us in—and there really wasn't no contact with the officials of the prison camp down there—just locked us in and kind of left us on our own. Now, in Marion, when they put a fence around the jail, they put all of us in there and locked some of us in the jail, and outside the jail. And that was a little bit more intimidating than Selma was in the prison camp.

How many days did students march and do sit-ins?

Just one day. The next week was the week that Jimmy Lee Jackson got shot. 'Cause the Movement—we started having meetings every night at the church in Marion. After the sit-ins and stuff. And they were planning some more activities in Marion when Jimmy Lee Jackson got shot at night. We had a meeting—a rally at night in Marion. The rally was over with about eight or nine o'clock. And the people just—some of 'em went down to the café and club down at the back of the church, and they were just hanging around town—a large group of them, and I was sitting with a great-uncle at the hospital.

That night about 10 o'clock, they brought Jimmy Lee Jackson out to the hospital. And they put him in the hallway at the front of the hospital and he was crying in pain and stuff. And the nurse and stuff, get 'em back in a group back in the room and stuff, talkin' 'bout they wasn't gonna wait on no niggas and stuff, and he stayed out there about two, two and a half hours before they transported him to Selma. But the nurses and doctors in Marion wouldn't do anything for him.

What made you go to the hospital that night?

I was spending the night with my great-uncle. Jimmy Lee Jackson's grandparents went to the same church as we did—that's where they were . . . in Sprott, Alabama—a little community. And everybody knowed and everything—and Granddad and Mother and everything were from Sparks, and that's where my great-uncle were. And my mother and stuff were from Sprott. And that's where my great-uncle was from. And I was sitting with him at night because his grandson took care of him. And he worked during the day, so I went to school during the day, and we went to the rallies at night, and after the rallies and stuff I would go to the hospital and spend the night. And that's what had me out at the hospital that night.

Were you ever—were young people allowed at the mass meetings?

Yeah. In fact, the majority of the participants were young people—students. Like I said, the Movement—all the activity of the civil rights movement in Marion was carried on by students. And didn't have but a few adults that participated in the Movement. Adults stayed on white folks' land, and they was prohibited from participating. And just like my uncle and my wife, they were ran off the place where they stayed after the civil rights movement. So, they—the people that had five other places to stay, and it was like Webb, one community on another side of town. Sprott was on one side of town on the southeast side and on the northwest side of Marion is Webb. And Webb has all the people that stayed—all the blacks stayed on his place—they participated. They were half the Movement.

Oh, so Webb was the name of—is that a community?

Yeah, Webb—he owned—it was a plantation, Like Sprott have

a post office. It was a plantation, but it had a post office there—it has the name of Sprott and it is listed as a city.

Alright, so I didn't realize that's how it worked. I didn't know that's how it worked.

Yeah—anywhere there was a post office, they had a name of a city.

And that's how it was for Webb, too? Webb was considered a city? Did it have its own post office?

Webb didn't have a post office. But there was a big plantation and they just had a lotta blacks that stayed out there. And him—Jeff Jones—white—hung together—Webb, Jeff Jones, Sprott, and most plantation owners stuck together and what one said, the rest of 'em said. So, when they had they little meetings and decided that the only thing they could do to fight the civil rights movement was to run the blacks off they land.

And they participated. And, like, Jeff Jones did it—on 14 between Selma and Marion, he had a plantation down there on 14 and he had all these blacks run off that participated. When he got through he didn't have but one family on the farm. And Webb and the rest of 'em, they threatened blacks, but they didn't carry it out because of the fact that they didn't have anybody else to work their farm.

Yeah, that's what I'm thinking—if they run people off the farm they don't have anybody else to work.

And afterwards, a lot of 'em lost their farms and stuff. Due to the fact that they couldn't support the farm without blacks. And Jeff Jones was one of 'em.

Is he the one that your great-uncle worked for?

No, he worked for Sprott.

Jeff Jones set on 14 and about sixty white plantations are in the area.

That are still there right now?

Uh, most of 'em, yeah. Because what they do now, they lease out the land.

And like, at Sprott, the daughters was still living all during this time, and they ran blacks off the farm. But they son, one lady had a son and one of 'em had a daughter, and they still stay down there. The son, Luther—he stayed down on 14. And when I go down and see him, we talk. And some of the Sprott estate, they had whites as well as blacks that stayed on Sprott's estate. And, my uncle, 'bout my age—he and one of the whites that we was raised up with, they went into the army together.

Was it Vietnam?

No, it was during the Vietnam time, but they didn't go to Vietnam. They was in the army together, stationed together. They've become good friends. And his sister visits my grandmother—up 'til she died. And, some of the whites became good friends with blacks and stuff.

Was it the younger ones that typically became good friends?

Yeah.

Was that ever true of the older generation?

No, the older generation—they tried to hold onto the old ways and stuff. There's a little juke joint off of 5—at the intersection of 5 and 14.

Hmm—I've probably driven by it.

It's on the . . . it's kind of a "y"-shaped road there. . . . It's Highway 5 and 14 going to Marion. It's a service station and a restaurant and stuff. . . . If you been to Marion you went in that-a-way coming from 5 from Birmingham, or you turned right there at the intersection. It's a juke joint back over there—and they still hang out—the Klan—the group. One of them was supposed to have been so bad back during the civil rights movement, they had—this club there during that time, and that group stayed together, and they still hang out there today. And don't no blacks go in there. It's just all-white—a little juke joint.

Is there still Klan activity in Marion?

Yeah. Blacks run Marion now and they are not vocal or have any pull or anything, but they still have their little group and everything—and that juke joint is one of they strongholds. That's where they hang at. But after Jimmy Lee Jackson got shot, the activity moved to Selma—rallies and the Movement started concentrating on the march from Selma to Montgomery. And I was in Selma on Bloody Sunday.

You were there?

Yeah.

Can you tell me what that experience was like?

I was about twelve, fourteen rows from the front on Bloody Sunday and we had got an instruction—how to handle tear gas and stuff, because none of the people but the people from the civil rights movement that came in town had any experience with tear gas. So they had to tell us how tear gas would affect us and how to react to it—when they gon' start throwing tear gas, to kneel down and cover your face, and stuff. And so when we got there and they stopped us on the bridge, and told us to disperse, and they refuse, they start beating on the front of the line. And the horses and stuff started running back, down the line. And I was doing what I was instructed to do, and I kneeled down and I covered my face and stuff, and all of the noise, the hollerin' and everything going on around me, and finally I looked up, and I was there by myself.

Do What the Spirit Says Do

When they took the horses and stuff and started beating and pushing and beating back, the people started running back towards town—back towards across the bridge. And there was a tractor—farm equipment—down side where we was on the bridge—where we had just crossed the bridge. And tear gas and smoke and stuff was so bad, people were running down—down through the farm equipment—plows and stuff—and ran down in the river on that side. And once I got up, I moved back down to the side of the bridge and was about the cross the bridge back to the church. And I got in a group of ladies and cops followed me around trying to get the horses close—and the horse went swinging and hit me, and I dug down and ran down through the busy section right there, and I ran into one lady from my hometown, and we went and got in kind of an apartment and sat 'til later when everything quiet down. 'Cause see, after, we got back to the church—the projects around the church.

And in the process of them telling us what to expect and everything, it was some young guy taking some pictures and stuff, and they were talking 'bout how they wasn't gonna take no shit outta nobody. They had they guns and stuff, but when everything broke down and people started running back towards the church, they was some of the first ones that ran. And, um, once they got back in the projects and everything, they started shootin'.

And like I said we was in one of the apartments there, while the shooting and everything goin' on, 'til everything quieted down. But the cops and stuff, they stayed out of the projects.

Once they got back in the projects, they took a stand and they stopped running. They had run and chased us from the bridge all the way back to the projects. They were driving with horses and stuff and once they backed us in the project then, they took a stand, and that's when the shooting and stuff started. And the cops and stuff stayed out, especially after it got dark and stuff. And after it quieted down, and started getting dark, I went back to the church—me and Fannie Ford—everything quieted down, and they provided transportation back to Marion.

Oh okay. Did you go again? Did you go all the way to Montgomery?

Yeah, I marched all the way to Montgomery.

Wow—you're the first person who's told me what Bloody Sunday was like.

Yeah. It was . . . chaos. Because, like I said, when I finally got up, I was by myself. And the cops went around me just like when I was kneeling down. They were driving the crowd back 'cross the bridge. And they didn't hit me or attack me or anything. They just went around me. And then I raised up and seen that I was there by myself. I started running back toward the bridge. But when they hit me with that tear gas and stuff, people just running down through the tractor place there, down where there is farm equipment and stuff? People was getting hurt, running down on plows and stuff. Go behind tractors and stuff. They were running down through the area. And smoke and tear gas and stuff. And they were just running wild. And a lot of 'em got hurt.

And like I said, they were running down towards the river, some of 'em running into the river, because they just panicked. And they could tell you what to expect, but when them cops and stuff start beatin' 'em and no other stuff around 'em and everything, with the horses and stuff, a lot of 'em just panicked and ran back 'cross the bridge and back down through the projects and stuff. And once they got back to the church and stuff and got back in the projects, they took a stand.

When you look back on that experience now, what do you think and feel when you look back to those experiences?

It was a time that a lot of things came clear to me and everything, you know. How bad it was. Because the farm that I was raised up on—the plantation I was raised up on, we got along good. It was a group of white kids, and me and my uncle and them, it was about eight or ten of us. And we used to fight—white fighting blacks and stuff. And we used to beat them. The son of the plantation owner—we used to beat him up and stuff. The prejudice wasn't obvious to us. 'Cause like I said, it didn't ever come up.

So what made you, on the day that Lincoln High School, the day that all the students got off the bus and went towards town, what made you join? Were you just joining the crowd? Did you know what you were getting into?

I had listened to Dr. King and Abernathy speak that night before, and they had told us, of course, what they wanted us to do. So I [was] with him a hundred percent.

Is that what sparked your awareness of the prejudice?

Like I said, Bloody Sunday, and that night with Jimmy Lee Jackson and stuff, that's what opened my eyes up to how bad it really was, because like I said, where we were raised up and stuff, white and black played together, fought together, fought against each other, and nothing else came up of it.

Did your uncle ever talk about—your great-uncle—did he ever talk about discontentment? . . . Did he ever seem discontented or angry?

No. He had went up north and moved back some years before.

Oh, that's interesting.

And he was a barber, and he never talked about it. He was just quiet. Like I said, everybody got along good over at Sprotts. Wasn't no confrontation between black and white.

One time, a white family moved into Sprotts. A poor white family. They workin' for Sprott just like the blacks were. And they accused one black of raping a girl.

Did he live?

Yeah. He spent seven years in prison. He came out, and

somebody ran over him about a year after he was out of prison.

What? And it put him in the hospital, or he died?

Killed. They killed him. That happened—police had arrested him. He was a drunk. The weekend, Earnest—his name is Earnest Ford—and he was the drunk. He stayed drunk the whole weekend. Catch him on the highway, drunk. And they would take him to town and lock him up, and Monday morning, and they would let him out in time to be back to work. And they had locked him up that night before they said that happened. So, he was in jail and the state troopers say he had locked him up and say he was in jail during the time he was supposed to have molested this young girl. But the white folks got so aroused around town about it. They didn't care. They sent him to prison anyway. They didn't worry about whether he was there or not, it only mattered that he was accused of it. And they sent him to prison. And people that own the plantation and stuff, they ran the white family off that did it. They ran them off the place.

Oh, they did. They ran the poor white family that accused him off the place?

Yeah—it was just poor white trash. Troublemakers. And Earnest was harmless, and you know, nonviolent type. And everybody around there knows, and they know he didn't do it. And so after they went out, and they ran him off the place, and they made moves. And then like I said, when Earnest got out of prison, one night, they found him on the highway out there where somebody had ran over him.

Wow. Somebody was probably mad.

Yeah, because seven years for molesting a white girl wasn't no time. But it's a lotta time when you didn't do it.

But after I went through Marion down through the civil rights movement and everything, I became an activist for civil rights and stuff. And we marched and picketed against Sears. In Atlanta. Sears and Roebuck.

Oh, Sears . . . what were they doing?

They were discriminating against blacks in the workplace and stuff. In '72 we had striked against Sears here in Atlanta. And I was in the service department and I was the spokesperson for the service department. And the whole day they had us doing this time. And we got increase in pay, promotion, and stuff, all—Sears was a redneck company, and we marched back, and we started demanding equal work for equal pay and opportunities to get promoted were just for whites.

And so you achieved that.

Yeah.

Just so I get a bit of a timeline, when did you move to Atlanta?

I went into the service after I finished high school. Like I said, we graduated the last year of Lincoln High School.

What year was that?

Sixty-five.

Oh, you graduated in '65.

And Lincoln closed '66.

Oh that's right. You said that.

And, once you finished high school back then, you left Marion. 'Cause there wasn't nothin' there to do. So we went to Pennsylvania, and stayed with an aunt, and we volunteered and went in the service there. And we spent—me and my uncle spent three years in the service together. And after we got out, I came to Atlanta.

We always talk about, you know, what you don't know about don't bother you. 'Cause when we was growing up and, uh, working in the fields and stuff, you really wasn't aware that things was different in other places than it was on the farm.

Mmm. That is so interesting. And were all your brothers and sisters on the same farm? So nobody knew how bad it was?

No! We had a piece of car and stuff and went to school and went to games and stuff that the school participated in. And like I said, it wasn't bothering us that things were as bad as it was until the civil rights movement came in and then white folks started showing their true colors. But, uh, now, at Sprotts—my home church there in Sprotts, they had finished it, they built a new church about fifteen years ago.

And they want to expand. And a school sits on the same property that the church sittin' on. And the heir to Sprott's estate told my sister and them—Frances and them—that any land that they needed to expand the church and stuff, they free to use it. Take any land they want.

Really!

Yeah. And, um, Frances and the lady—one of the owners—one of the daughters of the owners of the Sprott estate—old man Sprott—Frances and my mother—they were good friends and stuff—Frances was a nurse and she took care of her when she was sick and dying. And the family kept a good relationship with Sprotts after the civil rights movement and everything went out.

Yeah, and like I said, the daughter, and, uh, granddaughter of old man Sprott, like I said, she told Frances and them that any land around the church that they want, they can take whatever they want to expand the church and stuff. And without any problems and stuff. And the Sprott's estate family kept a good relationship with the family. And, you know, um, they didn't never would do anything to just the family or any blacks around there during the whole civil rights movement.

You think they just had a different attitude? Or were they more grateful? Or what was the reason for it?

They had more of a different attitude. And, uh, back in there in the forties and fifties, they had—Sprott estate had a reputation of protecting they blacks.

Yeah. If a black went into town and got into trouble, if he could make it back across the river to the Sprott estate, he was good to go. They protected blacks like that. And they had a reputation, you know—if you made it back to Sprotts you were good to go, regardless of what you did.

But I think it was just old man Sprott. I ain't never know, he died before I was born. His daughter and wife, they was always 'round there. And my parents and grandparents worked for him. And they always had a good relationship with them, and during the civil rights movement and stuff, the relationship stayed there.

Wow. That's interesting. And so they didn't—they weren't running blacks off of their land—those who participated in the Movement.

No. It was Webb and . . . Jeff Jones.

It was a lotta of farms around there, you know, where blacks stayed and worked for . . . and those the ones that was running the blacks out.

[Pause]. So can you say a little bit more about Bloody Sunday? And there were two more attempts after that, right? To get to Montgomery?

Yes, Selma to Montgomery.

And what happened in the second attempt?

They had a bunch of white parishioners and church leaders and stuff.

Marching also?

Yeah. They were at the front of the line—a lot of cardinals and bishops and stuff.

It was a large group of white parishioners and stuff were at the front of the line with Dr. King and we went to start the march from Selma to Montgomery. And Johnson had put the National Guard on the highway and everything from that Sunday when we started the march all the way in to Montgomery. The National Guard was posted on the side of the highway.

And now going through you had whites that end section and stuff . . . be hollerin' "Hey nigga" this and "Nigga" that while we were marching. But they kept a distance. You know, because the National Guard was there. And that night, we had camp set up and everything. And movie stars and recording stars and stuff would visit at night. That's when I found out that uh *Bonanza*—Purnell? The one who plays Adam on *Bonanza*? That's an old show. The older son. Well, that's when I found out he's bald-headed. [laughs] 'Cause on the show he got a head fulla hair. And he had been on *Bonanza* all this years and stuff, and when I seen him down there in camp one night, that when I realized he was completely bald.

Who were some other celebrities?

Harry Belafonte, Jackie Wilson . . . there was a couple black women entertainers was there. Every night there was a group of entertainers and celebrities in camp.

The second attempt, the whole group marched for about fifteen miles—or they have a cutoff point where they only allowed three hundred past that point.

The crowd, probably about fifty thousand in there. Marching. And so they cut 'em down to three hundred. And it was all type of people from other states and stuff came to participate and then march. And like I said, at night they cut it down to three hundred and then they had camp set up every night as far as for sleep and stuff.

And so you were included in that three hundred.

Yeah.

Okay. Did they just stop it at a certain point in the line? Or—

They came down through the line and picked out a group.

Okay. And so, what happened on that second attempt? Why didn't the group go all the way?

We did! On the second attempt . . . we went all the way in.[2] And once we got inside of Montgomery, the group picked up more people would join in and we marched into Montgomery. A big march into Montgomery, to the capitol. And we had a big rally there at the capitol. Now, my sister was telling me the state of Alabama took a lot of pictures and stuff, of the civil rights movement, and they have 'em on display down in the capitol, in Montgomery and stuff—a lot of things that weren't covered by reporters on the civil rights movement, the white governor and all, the state of Alabama have pictures and stuff that they took during Bloody Sunday, and the march from Selma to Montgomery, and once we got in Montgomery, they had a lot of pictures and stuff that they took—the government did—and they put 'em in the capitol not too long ago. They on display.

And so, what took place after you made it to Montgomery? What happened just in the days following this when you came back to Marion? What was the mood in the town? What do you remember?

---

[2] There were actually three attempts to march from Selma to Montgomery, but it is likely that Mr. Dobyne only attended the first and third marches.

Walter Dobyne

Everything was kinda tense . . . in Marion, right after Jimmy Lee Jackson got killed and everything. There was a lot of tension in Marion, and after we marched Selma to Montgomery, there was still a lot of tension and stuff. It was years afterwards when things got relaxed and stuff started returning back to normal.

Was there an increase in violence that you remember or an increase in discrimination?

No. Afterwards, blacks gonna start standing up and speaking up and Albert Turner ran for political office in Marion. He was the first black that had a political office in Marion. And they started getting blacks on boards of education and the city council and county commissioner and stuff. But it took a while for the tension to relax in Marion.

Isn't it true that blacks didn't start being elected until the mid-seventies or so—is that accurate?

I can't remember exactly when he was elected, but he was the first one. And it seemed like in the sixties he was elected county commissioner. Because voter registration went on after the march to Selma to Montgomery and stuff, and Selma still had voter registration, and that was some tension there—whites didn't just roll over and die.

They had a shed down at Bull Connor, and he had something to say about blacks going in to register to vote and stuff. He would be standing outside of the courthouse and stuff. Different things to harass blacks and stuff. But in Marion, voter registration was a big push then, afterwards, to get blacks out get to 'em registered to vote.

And, was it the same then as it is now, that you had to be—how old did you have to be—twenty-one to register?

Yeah.

Okay. So you weren't able to register at that time.

No. It was just getting a parent to register to vote. It was a big push 'cause a lot of the blacks were still reluctant to come out and vote—and register and stuff. They'd have to kind of encourage them to go out and register to vote, but that's when everything turned—'til after the march from Selma to Montgomery over getting blacks registered to vote.

What was the mood at Lincoln High School after the march?

We had a principal that was hard-lined. And after the march—after we marched and everything, it took the bite out of his bark.

I want to move on to ask a different question. And these again are just clarifying what happened after the marches: You said that voter registration really increased during that time. And you talked about the tension that took years to dissipate, right? After the Movement, was there any other activity? Any other protesting that took place during the years . . .

No, like I said, voter registration—that was the big thing then. The next couple of years still, that's what the emphasis was put on—voter registration. And didn't have no major demonstration in Marion back then.

Were you aware of civil rights activity that was happening in other parts of the state in the time when you were in school?

Yeah—Birmingham. We kept up with everything going on in Birmingham, and the Movement there. My mother kept up with all of that. So, she kept us abreast of what was going on in Birmingham or something . . . and the Movement there. At home, it was a topic of what Dr. King was doing, and what they were doing in Birmingham.

And did you find that other students going to school with you—your peers, that they were informed? That they were well-informed of what was happening? Did they know what was going on in other parts of the state?

Well, believe it or not, before Dr. King came to town, there really wasn't no—any really discussion of the civil rights movement in Marion. It just bloomed up—the civil rights activists came to town, and everything just bloomed up in a week. And wasn't nothing that drug on and stuff . . . no, far as the students and everything. Round campus and stuff, never.

It wasn't something that you ever talked about.

No.

See, the story I've heard was that James Orange was standing outside the gates one morning and as students got off the bus, and they were going to go to school, he said to them, and this is a story I've heard from a couple of people: "You're not going to school today, but, you're gonna march."

I don't remember him being out there. 'Cause Martha Dixon was going from classroom to classroom, getting students out. And I was talking to the seniors in the senior class, trying to get them out. 'Cause the rest of them were seniors. But all the students came in to the classrooms and we left out of the classrooms and left off-campus.

Okay. Well, I'm sure a couple of different . . .

Well, I'm saying he could've been down there because I was on campus, in the classroom, and the students that I talked to and everything, trying to get 'em out, was in the classroom.

Okay. Alright. That makes sense.

Now Orange, he was in Marion, and he had been [inaudible] the Movement and stuff, and training, and working with the students and stuff, but like I said, I just don't remember him being there. Because we were all students . . . involved. Everything I remember, it was just students. It wasn't no adults involved in it.

Well, I think—well, we've been talking for just about an hour and thirty-two minutes, and I feel satisfied with what you have shared with me. And again, is there anything else that you think should be told about Marion from that period that you would like to make sure you include, or you feel pretty comfortable with what you have shared?

The only thing I don't want—don't think enough emphasis put on students were the ones who actually started everything. The civil rights movement actually was in town—they organized everything, but the ones on the frontlines was students. 'Cause the sit-ins and everything that happened, in Marion, wasn't no adults taking part—it was all students taking part and doing the sit-ins and the white establishment and stuff. And Orange and Tyrone Brooks and them organized and issued money and tell you where to go.

But the students were the ones who were actually taking the risks and going into these places and . . .

Yeah.

Well, I thank you for taking this time.

Okay.

Edward Daniel

Edward Daniel, the first black mayor of Marion, discusses his time at the Lincoln Normal School as a high school coach, mentor, and teacher, lending some insight into life there after schools were integrated. He also lends some insight into the social realities in Marion during the 1960s—black/white relations and gender relations within the black community. Mayor Daniel also offers his recollections of the civil rights movement in Marion, including the all-important youth movement led by James Orange.

□ □ □

I know you weren't born and bred here, but can you remind me of how you became a resident of Marion?

Well, I took a job teaching at Lincoln. My very first year here I was at Marion Baptist Academy. That was that school that I think Reverend Bryant and I was up there the day you were here before, because a volunteer church had come, and they were doing some renovations on that Baptist training building. And that's where I worked the first year. The next year, the basketball courts moved up to the principal at the high school, and the superintendent moved me to Lincoln, which was the high school.

And what year was that?

Well, the first year I was here was 1959. I moved to Lincoln in 1960. And that was the reason. Personally, I just took a teaching job to get about two years of experience and go back to Birmingham.

And you ended up staying twenty-eight years.

Ended up staying thirty-five years in the school system. Because when I became mayor I continued to teach. But I just didn't coach anymore, 'cause it would have taken too much time for me to coach and teach and be mayor. And my wife worked at Lincoln—let's see . . . that was my third year, 'cause she came in 1962. And that's when we met.

And she taught what grade level?

She taught basically the ninth grade—it was Alabama history and civics. And they've dropped both of those courses now, and I can't understand why they would drop Alabama history—if you're in Alabama, lived in Alabama, raised in Alabama, born in Alabama, at least you ought to want to know something about the state. But, that was part of the renewing of the curriculum.

So, tell me just broadly speaking, tell me about your recollections of being a teacher at Lincoln School.

Oh, it was wonderful. I don't know how smart the principal was, but he ran a good school. You know, wasn't no crazy stuff goin' on—children were disciplined. And that was not only the principal, but that was comin' down from the parents also. We had an unwritten policy that you had to stay in the community at least two weekends out of the month, and that purpose was for you to at least attend church, and finagle in the community with different people, and people period. And I thought that makin' of a good school when the people that was runnin' the school system, they'd go among the people, don't separate yourself from the people. In two weeks I knew every child I taught, by name. And I also connected with every child, and who they were, as far as parents. Some of 'em I could tell by how they look, 'cause they look a lot like their parents. Some I could tell through their attitudes . . . and then a lot of 'em I had coached in the athletic program. Some of 'em used to tell me, "Put a broom on that boy, Coach!" I said, "I didn't put a broom on you, so I'm not gonna start with your son! That's your job.

They hired me to coach—they didn't hire me to beat up on kids!" And that guy would have been the first one to sue me if I had struck his kid. I knew better than that. Some coaches didn't know. I didn't think it took all that doggin' kids anyhow. Hell, if you want 'em to do something, teach 'em well.

So, that was your philosophy in terms of teaching?

Well, sports was just another phase of teaching. I mean, you'd be surprised how once you try to start teaching children, how well they can get down into the bottom part of their mind. I got kids right now, in their sixties; call me from Los Angeles; from Chicago; from Fort Wayne. One called me the other day tellin' me about his retirement party—this guy was turning sixty-seven, and he remembered as much about me as I know about myself. He told me, he said, "You know, in raising my children, I used a lot of the rules and regulations that you passed down to us." And that make you feel good.

Like what, for example?

Well, like, "Don't cheat. Don't lie. Don't steal." Just basic, fundamental things that anybody ought to wanna know. And we had a good time. And I tried to fit every child who wanted to go to college to some school I thought they could make it in academically, even if I had to drop down to the junior college level. And some of 'em ended up in junior college, and ended up with a degree! And other teachers would tell 'em, you won't make it, or, you don't have enough to make it. You not disciplined enough. But what they did have was the "want to." I "want to" do this. And it's amazing how other children will pattern after children who want to do something good. And I tell the teachers—I say, if you show some interest in this child, you'd be surprised how much—and I used to talk about things like DNA——I'd say, this kid is doing well because some of his cousins, or some of his uncles, or aunties did well.

And they looked at that and think they're supposed to do well. And some of 'em did do well as a result of knowing who some of their background relatives were. And I used to make sure I told 'em those things. 'Cause some of 'em, the parents didn't tell them. And I know, the problem a lot of time with parents—they busy working! They're try'na feed those kids! They're try'na clothe those kids! I told a teacher that one day. She was just raisin' all kinds a hell because the kids had been cutting up. I said, "You ever tried to go over this child's house? Just go over there, and see where he come from!" Boy told me—he said, "We stay hungry." He said, "My momma don't get up and cook breakfast before we leave for school." I went to the principal, and I guess he thought I was crazy. I said, "Listen—when the lunch hour is over, can I have all the leftover food?" And he didn't know what I wanted with it. I explained to him that some of my players looks like they had given out by the halftime. And I said, "That's a sign that they not gettin' enough food." They don't have enough energy. We turned that program around when we started feedin' those kids. Right after school we would take those kids back into the lunchroom. You know, in a quiet way—I didn't want the other kids knowing about it. And their performance improved at least 30 percent.

Let me get back on task.

That's okay. You made a comment a little earlier that teachers were required to stay on campus—is that right? Stay at the school.

They did have a boarding area for lady and men teachers.

Okay, yes. But you were saying that they had to be integrated into the community somehow.

Yes.

And at this time were the teachers all black?

No—might've had a few whites sprinkled in.

And other recollections of your days at Lincoln School? Particularly leading up to—

I loved Lincoln School. Show you how much I loved it, the first seventeen years I was in the system, I didn't miss a day. I got up and went to work. Seventeen years. So, but my first year in Marion, I started out with a good principal. We called him Professor Tubbs. He was a little sparky guy—looked like a Marine. But he didn't care who you were. If you did wrong, he was gonna whip you! He even threatened to whip some teachers!

But he was a tough guy. I guess he was about fifty. And I was about twenty. But I learned a lot from him. Said if you tell a child something, stick with what you told him. But make sure you tellin' them something that's right. Something that the parents can work out and agree to and they'll support you.

And what do you think it was about the education at Lincoln School that made a difference in the community?

Well, I think it kind of instills something in children to let them know if you work hard, you will succeed. A lot of young men and women too—young ladies—the biggest area that the children went into was nursing, and then teaching . . . from a professional point of view. A lot of 'em ended up in places like Detroit and Cleveland and Fort Wayne and all, because they got jobs with the automotive industry and they worked. I mean, they stayed there thirty and forty years of working on those jobs. And some of 'em bought homes, and some of 'em raised their children well and sent their children to college. Some of 'em didn't get a chance to go to college themselves, but they made sure their children went. 'Cause they had good income, and they saved their money and they budgeted their money to the point where they could pay their children's way to school. And we were real tickled at that. That was a success story within itself. The children whose momma and daddy didn't have two pair of pants, or a pair of stockings, if they went to something grown-up like. And, I still try to relate to some of the children that's coming through school now even though I don't teach—that who their relatives were and what some of 'em are doing now, and what they tried to do even prior to getting to the point where they are at. More children came through Lincoln that ended up with PhDs than any other school in the nation. Horace Mann Bond did this documentary on blacks with PhDs and that's what he discovered.

And that's of any black school in the nation?

Any black school in the nation. That was a tremendous success story.

I remember, you told me that last time, and that is amazing.

And I think it made us work harder as teachers. I see people now they talking about want to retire after about five years. After five years they talking about retiring. I say, if you retire guess what they going to replace you with? Another white teacher. And so you lose ground. You're not going to be that role model that you could be by staying on. I said I know you get tired, and I know that there are some children that are contrary. But teach 'em anyhow. Teach them anyhow. And when the schools integrated, I think some of those years that I didn't stay off from work was the fact that there were some teachers that were just fretful. If they found out certain teachers weren't in school, they think they should be at home. "I don't know whether or not I can handle that classroom knowing that Mr. so-and-so not here today." And they have that in the back of their mind. He'll get up and teach! Demand something, but be fair about it.

I think when the school system first integrated it was about 50 percent black and 50 percent white. Then the whites—I don't know what happened. But a lot of 'em decided, well, we're gonna pull our kids out and start a private school.

And that's Marion Academy?

Well, it was Marion Academy, and those who could afford it was Marion Institute. And that was very expensive. Well, to be honest, Marion Academy was expensive, based on more than 50 percent of the white students. Parents didn't have nothin'. But they didn't understand when they thought about startin' up a school system—run a school system like it's supposed to be. They didn't have no money.

Hmm . . . that's interesting. The white parents didn't have money. And they didn't understand how expensive it is to run a school.

That's right.

But they just knew that they wanted to pull their kids out.

And they really didn't have any serious reasons. 'Cause we didn't have that much of a discipline problem where white kids were afraid of black kids.

So it was really motivated by parents.

My athletic teams were about as integrated as you could get. I did notice a peculiar thing, and I knew why. My football team was pretty much 50 percent black and 50 percent white. My basketball team was 90 percent black and 10 percent white. My baseball team was 90 percent white and 10 percent black. And then I start looking at it and studying it: white kids had the opportunity in their communities to play Little League baseball. There wasn't much of a Little League baseball team in the black community. But they played a lot of basketball. You know, it's about all the yards spread out and had a goal in it—so they played a lot of basketball. They played football because—I say because it was the beginning of school. Football started up when the school start up, so a lot of kids would come out. When I first got there, only black kids the white coach wanted was a super athlete. He didn't want to be bothered with the rest of the kids.

He didn't want to train them up.

Yeah. And the kids weren't no fool! They recognized all he wanna do is fool with the ones of us who were superstars.

So they walked out on him one day. He didn't want me to . . . the first two years I was assistant football coach. He didn't want me to do that. He used to say, "Come to the field this afternoon and help us tape whoever the kids are injured ankles, and then sit up in the stands and watch the practice." That's what he told me. I never showed up. So then, he went runnin' to the superintendent, so then the superintendent called me in and told me what he did. He had said that I wouldn't cooperate with them as far as practicing, and then I just told the superintendent what the issues were. I said, I can't deal with a guy who won't even take the paper down from his face even when he's sittin' in the desk—in the dining room with his wife! He didn't even look at her! I knew things like that. Say he would put the paper up in front of him, and she's sittin' over there to eat breakfast—he was just that mean. He was just that mean.

In terms of the entire athletic department, was he over you?

Well, he never told me, and it killed him when he found out that I had become the football coach. The first two years I was just head basketball coach. And when he found out that I was the head football coach, he left. Didn't tell anybody. Just left. Well, even the white kids had dropped off the team. I think we had gotten down to about thirteen players. So the superintendent came and asked me would I consider becoming the football coach. I said no, I wouldn't consider that because those kids have a losing attitude. And I said, I don't think I could make chicken salad out of chicken shit! [laughter] He said, well, don't give me an answer now. Tell me sometime next week. So in between that time I asked all the kids—all the boys—that if I ever became the football coach, would they come out and play. Well, 70 percent of the kids said yeah. But I wasn't no fool, now. I know some of 'em who said yeah wasn't gon' come out. And, I did—I ended up with about fifty kids. I said to myself, and out of that fifty, some of them were tremendous, good athletes who had never played no football, but they were good athletes. So I said to myself, I said I can take these fifty kids and make an outstanding team out of it. And I did! We won the first seven games we played that year. Lotta coaches who knew me was telling me things like—and I probably woulda done this different had I had a successful program in the beginning—if a kid don't come out when we tell 'em we startin' practice, I won't let 'em play after that. I said, "Well, you defeatin' yourself! 'Cause you sure have to have these kids! If you don't have the kids, how can you have a good team?" So . . . and the kids were watchin'—they were watchin' me and watchin' the team: "If he's successful, we'll go out and play!" You know, and the parents were the same way. They would call me at night, 'cause they didn't want nobody to know they were talkin' to me. "Uh, my kid wanna play football—is it too late for him to come out?"

These were white parents.

These were white parents.

"Is it too late for them to come out?" [laughs] It was like a little game with me. Yeah.

Wow—so it's not like all the parents pulled all the kids out of the school, or did it become that way eventually?

Well, it came to be . . . I'd say 95 percent.

By what year, would you say?

Uh . . . 1976–77. 'Cause I had a great team in everything. '72, '73, '74. We were playing in the state playoffs, and the kids wanted to—you know, they stick their chest out because we're gonna be playing over at the University of Alabama and so, I wasn't no fool, I knew how kids talk 'cause I knew how I talked. Yeah.

So, tell me, going back a little bit about '65—I'm thinking about what both you and Reverend Bryant told me about when I was here, and I wanted to get a little bit more detail on that. When the children were the ones who marched initially? Tell me about that period of time.

This was tough days for blacks. Because a lot of 'em worked for whites. So what happened, the black parents knew they would be fired right away if they got involved directly with the civil rights movement. They got involved with the meetings and stuff like that . . . 'cause they stuck by their kids, they wasn't gonna let nobody just run over their kids, or beat up on their kids or nothin' like that. But the thing was, children were very active and they were aware of what was going on in the sixties. And when you bring somebody in like a Martin Luther King, and the other people that were surrounding him as speakers, I think you can convert a lot of kids.

Did children attend those [mass] meetings?

Oh yes, pastors attended them more so than children. Children got involved in the daytime meetings, where they would go to Selma and march. And march in Marion . . . they were both involved with the marches as far as the parents and the children. Yeah. What they would do—they would ride the bus to school, and then get off the bus, and wherever they're supposed to meet up for a march, a meeting, that's where they would go. And they would come back to the school about the time they thought the buses were there.

So does that mean the schools were empty?

Pretty much. Pretty much. I'd say more than 80 percent of the children would be gone.

And did the children initiate this?

Well, they had organizers. And they were people that the children looked up to. They were tough people. They were people who would talk back to white people, and the children were just . . .

Do you remember the first time that happened? That the children left school in order to protest?

Oh yes. See we would have various duties. Like, one week you might have school bus duty, so you're right out there—you don't have to be involved by sayin' nothing. But just your eyes, you know—the children know Mr. so-and-so havin' bus duty today and he gon' see me as part of the Movement . . . and that kinda gave the children some kind of status. And then they got parents who would be at the meetings at night, more so than the children and sometimes they were mingling, or both. 'Cause a lot of singing went on and hand-clapping and, you know, activity tends to stir people up, draw people, and then they begin to hear names of people who were outstanding like Martin Luther King gon' be here tonight—well you know it's gon' be a packed church. And then there were other—all kinds of other important people. They found their way to Marion, 'cause Marion was a very active town as far as civil rights.

And so the day that—the first day that you remember that children got off the bus, what happened?

Well, quite naturally, everybody's wondering, "Where the children?" If you were on bus duty, you knew where they were. And gotten off the bus, and people told 'em which way to go and where to meet, and they did that. They asked the teachers not to get directly involved, so they couldn't just bring some kind of action against you, like fine you—yeah.

And—well, I've heard this name quite a bit—James Orange, is it?

There's a statue out there by the old jail. He died recently. Not last year—I can't be exact. But the last two or three years. Children liked him. Very much. He represented a strong man. And I guess people like Martin Luther King needed great organizers. Make your job easier if they know—if your followers know exactly what you wanna do and how you wanna do it.

His—Dr. King's—thoughts were nonviolent, like Mahatma Gandhi. People liked that. He studied their ways, and methods, and he felt like if you put yourself in a position where you got to fight back to defend yourself, then you're defeating your purpose. You not gonna get other folks—a lot of other folks came in from other places—black and white—to assist with the Movement.

Hmm—a lot of people came to Marion specifically to assist?

Yes. Yes. See, Lincoln, long before the civil rights movement, had white teachers at Lincoln. They were Congregational Church members, come in from New York and Massachusetts and Connecticut and faraway places like that, who just knew what was going on in a lot of these southern places was not right. We used to get books that had a hundred pages torn out, but that's what they said was "separate but equal" [laughs]. Oh, I used to just . . . I don't know . . . I had a white lady to call me one night. She thought her son was supposed to be the most valuable player. She didn't address me. She was addressing the assistant coach. That's who she was mad with. 'Cause he was white, so she thought that he was supposed to hold up for her child, as far as the most valuable player.

So she didn't go to the head coach, but the assistant head coach.

Well, so, she called me, I guess about 11 or 12 o'clock that night. I could tell she had been drinking, 'cause her speech was slurred. And I could hear her husband telling her what to say to me in the background.

She calls you at home?

Yeah. But what really ticked me off . . . "You all just prejudice 'gainst my boy!" I said, "Ma'am— 'You all just prejudice 'gainst my boy'?" I said, "Lady, let me tell you what prejudice is. Have you ever ridden on the back seat of the bus?" When I start citing some stuff like that, she eased the phone down. I tickled myself. I ask her, "Have you ever drunk from a colored water fountain?" [laughs] She just didn't know what to say! "This man must be crazy!" Oh boy, I just tickled myself.

So, she just hung up after that?

Oh, she hung that phone up. And then ended up being one of the nicest followers of our athletic program.

Is that right? Wow! So she kept her child in the school?

She kept her child in the school! Daughter was a cheerleader. [laughs]

Wow! Even after it integrated?

Oh yes.

Maybe you sparked something in her!

Well, I think she was two people in one.

That's an interesting way to put it.

I would make sure I was cautious with her. 'Cause I wasn't gonna get hemmed up in a situation where he attack me. Yeah, so—a lot of 'em had to get used to . . . there are intelligent black people.

And it was obviously something that—why people resisted.

Oh yes, absolutely.

How would you describe the ways in which the black community bonded together, or, banded together, during the more difficult years?

Well, let's be honest, a lot of 'em were related. That go a long ways, you know. They would see a time to attack—blacks would attack other blacks, but they were upset if they heard of a white attacking another black. And I couldn't ever figure that out. You know, somebody hittin' you in the head with something, black or white that's hittin' you, it's hittin' you! [laughs] But you know I understood how they were handling it, and a lot of 'em did it well.

So it was the fact that there were such blood ties between blacks?

I would think so, even if some of 'em didn't go along with integration.

Some didn't?

Some didn't. They didn't openly fight against it.

Hmmm—why do you think there were some who were against integration?

Well, their fear. Their fear of the white man. Yeah.

And this is integration in general? Or just in the school system?

Integration in general. We always said it started at the church. We said the church is the most segregated place you could be at the 11 o'clock hour. And, I had a coach at the white school ask me one day, "Can I, come to some of your games?" I said, "Yeah—feel free to come!" He said, "Well, why don't you come to some of mine?" And before the day was out he was callin' me and tellin' me, "I don't think it was a good idea for you to come to my games."

Why is that?

'Cause he was sayin' there was some prejudiced white people. [laughs] See, he didn't have to tell me that.

Did he go?

No. He came to one or two [games], and next thing I looked up and see the superintendent is there. And he said to me, "You do a good job with your kids. I like coming to your games." And a few more started coming. And then when we went to the state tournament, the whole town came! [laughs] They were people that would've never come to Lincoln to a game—and then they got the whole town there.

But this was something they could brag about. The fact that our kids were winning, they didn't care.

And when was this? This was in the mid-seventies?

This was '69, '70, '71.

Okay, wow—that's a big deal! And the team was integrated at that point?

Not as much as we should have been.

But they came out because they were in the state tournament?

Oh yes. [Laughs] It was kinda funny to me. We used to—my friends and I used to laugh about it. You know, we used to get among ourselves and just laugh about it. Yeah.

Um, tell me a little bit more about the sense of community—again, during the more difficult years in the sixties. How did people help one another? How did people cope with the difficulties that the community was facing?

Some of 'em left—population started dropping off because, as I said, a lot of 'em farmed for the white people. They almost run the farm—run the plantation. And that made them feel good. Others had a difficult time. A lot of 'em that left had a difficult time. Most time their children—adult children—were eighteen, seventeen, twenty. They would leave. Girls too. 'Cause the white man wanted to finagle with black girls. But yet, he was sellin' the thought to his race and other race too that "I hate blacks." You got somethin' like that right now. Sure have, in fact, it's really broken down right here in Marion. And don't go to Bibb County—you'll see so many interracial children that you'll say, "Is this what segregation was about?" And it's open now. These white grandmothers don't try to hide it when they carry their grandchildren to Walmart. They hold 'em by the hand.

And they say, "How this change come about?"

And how is that different back then when white men were messing with black girls and they were giving birth to interracial children?

Well, he treated his wife just like she was a Negro woman. You better not say anything. And some of 'em even put their girlfriends ahead of their wives. White men had all kinds of—whatever you might call it. Some people might call it—

Power.

Yeah, power. Not strength, but power.

Abusing their power.

And it's amazing, how some of them are ownin' their black relatives. They show up at the funerals now. I said, "Wow," you sit back and you think of these things in your mind, and you say, "How did this happen? How did that happen?"

Today they outright and say, "Yeah, that's my brother by my grandfather." I'll say, "Gosh." [paused] Oh we could write books. [Laughs]

You should. Have you ever written a book?

Not really.

Have you thought about it?

Well, I've had some people to encourage me to do that, but I don't know. I just never took up on it.

I mean, even that subject in and of itself—you're the first person to bring it up. It's really interesting for me to hear about the extent to which that was going on in the sixties and even today.

Oh yes.

And the attitudes in the community towards it—the secrecy and those kinds of things are of interest to me as well. And how they impact social relationships and trust between blacks and whites during that time.

Oh yes. I say, you just go to some things—don't say nothin'—just look—observe and you'll be surprised at how so many things just come to light. And as I said, some of 'em just feel like it's time to just own up to what it was.

Do you still think there's a lot of secrecy and shame?

No. I don't. It might be a small percent of it, but so many folks have interrelationships . . .

Interracial relationships here?

Oh yes. Well, they try to have things together—one lady on Washington Street—she was just try'na call what they—some kinda tea—they let some things slip out. Fifty-fifty as far as race. And they get along well. I go just for observation purposes. I get invited to things and sometimes it's worrisome 'cause they don't think enough of people with the same status I have to invite them. And sometimes it's a lack of communication.

Tell me more about being a black man in Marion during that period of time. . . . How would you characterize the relationships with white men, and any specific memories you have that would illustrate your observations?

Well, there were some black men had courage, strength, and the white man knew *I better not fool with this guy. He's mean—he'll hurt me.* But to tell it like it was, that's the kind of guy that will hurt anybody! He'll hurt his own folks if you fool with him. And, white man knew that. They passed the word on down, "Don't bother with such-and-such person." And they had good ties with other white men.

By saying "good ties," what do you mean?

Well, "good ties" is when you can get somebody to do something that's not their thought and ideas.

That's interesting.

Oh yes.

That is really interesting—the social ties and relationships. Another topic that I'm interested in is forms of resistance, and some of the ways that blacks resisted against white power.

Well, once black people started to figure out how the white man tried to play you, then they used that strategy against them. Like borrowing money. You go and borrow money from somebody else, they got you over a little barrel now, if you can't afford to pay that money back. They kinda—you need some kind of economic base, and a lot of folk get themselves in a bind, how folk get you in a situation where they can almost socially force you to do things that you don't want to do. It bothered me when one guy turned his daughters over to a white man just for a few dollars. You go without.

Did that kind of thing happen often?

I'm sure it did, but they kept it low-key.

I didn't even know that kind of thing happened.

Oh yes.

And of course, that destroys the girls, and then it destroys the family relationship

Well, those kind of situations the person—the people end up leaving Marion. Some of 'em never come back and some come back once they can get to an age and time where they can handle a situation like that. Some people can't handle a situation like that. So that's why you had some unsolved murders—a person just go so far and so long trying to take something, and then they just commit a crime just to get around it or get over it or whatever.

What were some of those other moments of strength that you can recall? What were some of the other ways in which black people, particularly black men, resisted?

Well, to show some strength, a lot of 'em combined or united themselves with another church—black church groups. And that became a source of strength. They would meet up in the same places, and because of ties with the church, they had more than themselves to depend on.

What was your source of strength?

I felt like being from Birmingham, I could be a little different from folks that was from here.

How so?

I don't know—we had about five or six men—might have been more than that—from the Birmingham area that was teaching here. And we kind of formed us a little—without any hoorah . . . hooray . . . any excitement about it, we formed ourselves a little group. And we stuck together. If there were times when we had to go to Selma, we would let each other know, and try to encourage somebody else to go along with us—whether it was a social event or educational event, or sporting event or whatever, and even the black community restricted that. Those guys stickin' together. Just don't bother with them. And we didn't make no lotta noise about it.

So they were really your social support system.

Somewhat. I had a strong support system because my athletic program bonded a lot of other people with me. And they used to tell me, if you run into any problems, with such-and-such a person, let us know. And, well, I already knew who would give you a problem. And most time it would be a problem when a woman's name would come up. So don't bother with other folks' women.

Tell me more about that—what do you mean?

Well if there was a popular woman out there in the community that was just lookin' for something, don't even bother with those kind of women, I mean, just tell 'em, look, let them know that you're not interested, 'cause I can see how that could become a problem either with black on white or black on black.

Oh, but they were talking specifically about a popular white woman that may have been looking for something?

Most time it would be a popular black woman that maybe had a relationship with a white man. Every now and then a white woman's name would come up.

Hmm—that's interesting.

Those were the kind of white women who knew they had this white man tied up in such a way that he wasn't gonna raise too much hell. If he raised any hell, it would be with other white folks.

I just wouldn't allow white women to be followin' me. I had a group of 'em. Um, I kept it strictly athletic, they wanna wipe the kid's face—if they sweatin' and all that kind of stuff. And I'm not sure . . . most of them wasn't from Marion. They were people who had taken a job teaching. And, I don't know, I know white folk knew or what they were doing as far as black men—black boys. But we used to . . . myself and some of my friends, we used to get in behind closed doors and laugh about it. 'Cause these women thought—they thought that we were thinking they just doing this because they wanna help. They were socializing. But it was a way for them to grow in stature, and status. Oh, some of 'em would give their credit cards to black boys. So I just used to tell 'em, boy, they don't know what you doin,' now.

These are older black women who—

Oh yeah.

—who would give their credit cards—

Older white women.

—who would give their credit card to black boys—

That's right. And sometimes—

For what purpose?

This was the way they were gettin' close to 'em! And sometimes it would be white and black women.

*Author's note: This interview ended abruptly because we ran out of time and Mayor Daniel had to leave for another appointment. We were unable to schedule another time to continue the interview.

Eleanor Drake

Eleanor Drake, white female, employee of Judson College in Marion and longtime resident of Uniontown, Alabama, discusses the racial atmosphere in Uniontown during the 1960s, from the perspective of a homemaker with three small children. She talks about the school system, desegregation, the old mills, and her perspective on race relations in Uniontown during the Movement.

☐ ☐ ☐

I have very little knowledge of the period of the sixties except what you heard on the television 'cause at that time I had small children and I was working—I either worked in Demopolis or Uniontown, so I had very little contact with this part of the county.

So, my husband was in business in Uniontown. He worked in a grocery store, but our experience down there was entirely different. 'Course we're about twenty miles west of Selma and then twenty miles south of Marion. And we know what the papers had to say and what the television had to say about what was happening. And there was nervousness and people really didn't know what to expect. However, Uniontown experienced something entirely different than these other areas, because the people who boycotted Marion and Greensboro and Selma, came to Uniontown.

So, I'm kind of in a different position 'cause I saw a different side of it. Other than the fact that—I guess you could say that probably the white citizens of Uniontown were on edge because even at that time there was probably—the blacks probably outnumbered the whites three to one. So you know, if trouble had begun we would have been, you know, we would have been a great minority. We would have been greatly in the minority. But like I said, we didn't have problems. The merchants adjusted. Well, we only had one drugstore, and it immediately—well, the drugstore had a soda fountain, but it was open to blacks and whites immediately and—and restaurant wise, I don't even know that we had a restaurant. I'm not even sure what was there at that time. But, um, we went through it without a blemish.

So there was no civil rights activity in your town?

Mmm-mmm. Not to my knowledge—'cause I had three small children and a job and a husband. But it was really not—like I said, there was nervousness, and so—I saw an entirely different side. Like I said, people came there to do their shopping so it helped the merchants.

About how large was Uniontown in terms of population?

Probably two to three thousand—I mean you might have had about a thousand white and two thousand black. But it's still about the same today except you've got less whites today. So the percentages is probably 99 percent black to 1 percent white. But the ones of us who live there love Uniontown, so I'm not nervous in living there—I mean, you have to love a place to live there and to feel like that. So I guess, even though I'm not a Perry County native, Uniontown is home.

So Uniontown is in Perry County, but what part?

South . . . In fact, it's right on the edge of Perry and Marengo County. In fact, city limits now probably—they extended them probably, I think they go to the Hale County line just north of town, so now I grew up in Hale County, but I wasn't there when anything happened in Greensboro.

See the black citizens here [in Marion] were boycotting the merchants here, but they had to go somewhere to get groceries, so they would come to Uniontown.

The boycott, well, most of your stores—businesses were white-owned, so the black population—the blacks, like in Marion, were boycotting the white merchants and so they'd come to Uniontown—same thing happened in Selma and Greensboro, too, I think. So our merchants prospered for a while there.

So why do you think there was a comfort level coming to Uniontown?

That's kind of hard to explain. You'd have to—Well, I had a black man in Uniontown tell me one time—and I'm not real sure what he meant about the "peculiar relationships" between the blacks and whites in Uniontown. Now what he meant, I don't know—but there's been, over the years, a lot of talk people will say well, "I heard this is gonna happen and that is gonna happen," you know, as conflicts between blacks and whites, especially back in the sixties. It never happened. And evidently there—at that time, there was a feeling of—I don't know what the relationship was—but it just kinda [pause] . . . maybe people came in because they knew that, I don't know. I'd have to stop and think. And then probably [inaudible] because I'm not sure.

Were the relationships as you remember them? Did they appear peaceful?

Yeah! Back then—well I had small children back then and I had blacks in my home that kept my children while I worked. And there was no—well as far as the relationship between me and her—you know, I didn't think anything about it. I trusted her to take care of my children, and I guess she perceived that trust and I guess it goes back to the relationships. There were relationships back then that were not as they are now, 'cause all the strife and I don't know—in some ways, those are relationships that have been lost and that's the bad part about it. The good part is, there were good things that came out of it, but then the feelings of relationship between blacks and whites prior to that time is that, well, you took care of each other. I think that part is gone and I think that's bad.

And took care of each other in what way?

Well I can even remember my grandparents had a farm in Hale County. The people who worked for them could depend on them for food if they need it, they were clothed—I mean, you know, clothed. They were given a way to the doctor—but they showed an allegiance to them, too. It was a feeling of mutual dependence, and, I guess—and they just trusted each other. And that trust, I guess, is gone. But now, that's in a lot of relationships, not just blacks and whites today. I don't trust whites either, so . . . [laughter]

I have a tendency to this day to think well, look, am I reading this right or is there an ulterior motive, or, you know I just don't accept things at face value anymore, but that's just something that's developed over the years. That it was just a relationship and say what may have come probably out of the— I don't know—I'd hate to think that all of it was based on— well, I don't know—it was just a relationship that had lasted through the years between the two that is not here anymore. It's not there between whites and whites, and probably blacks and blacks.

Do you think that it was a necessary phase that these relationships had to go through, the breaking down of trust that happened in the sixties?

Well, probably so, 'cause I don't know that—never had thought about that and whether it was—for things to become . . . to do away with the old ways . . . Something had to go. So . . . you know, . . . I hope we have gotten to the point where we can start rebuilding some of it . . . but like I said, that's something, though, that's not just between blacks and whites, but whites and whites . . . and I'm sure, blacks and blacks. I don't . . . I don't accept anything at face value from most people. They'd have to be a really close friend [laughter] so . . . for me to accept that . . . you know, say, to rely upon someone else's word, it just really is not something that . . . that—I just can't accept people at face value anymore, whereas I used to. When I was young I didn't think anything about it . . . and that was maybe a young thing . . . may have been—instead of relying on something, blaming it on someone else. It may have been just the age, but I really think that some of the trust is gone that we had between each other.

I haven't heard anyone else so far talk about that, so it's a really interesting perspective that you're bringing.

Never thought about it being an interesting . . . It's just that [long pause] I have . . . some good black friends and some good white friends. It's like I said—I don't think that the relationships between—like they were back in the fifties and sixties will ever—probably not in my lifetime. I think it's probably to the point where it's going to depend upon the personal relationship with people instead of the blanket relationship that always seemed to be there. And like I said, that may be a growing-up thing, too.

In Uniontown—when desegregation happened, do you recall what took place at that time? And what your experience was—how you felt about the things that were taking place at that time?

Well now, my children started school at Uniontown Public School . . . one of 'em in '62, and one in '64, and the other one in—probably '69. Now, there were a few blacks in the system, say in '64 and '65, and it wasn't until late sixties, early seventies, really—and I think—I don't really know of any problems at the school—in the school system, and actually, in the white schools there, when it was all white, all your grades were in one building—first through twelfth grade, so you can see it was a small school, and all the white children went to what they call Uniontown High School, but it was first through twelfth. And then—they did have two schools that were black—an elementary and a high school. And at first there was only just one or two blacks in the school system. In fact, one of the first ones is an outstanding—I think he was a brain surgeon. I'm not sure where he is now, used to be in Tuscaloosa.

And I don't know that there was any trouble—and surely I would have 'cause mine were, say, third and fourth graders. But then, round the first part of the seventies, ours did go to a private school. Part of that was the fact that my oldest son had gone to kindergarten in Greensboro the year before we moved down here, and he had some cousins who were still in school in the public school system in Greensboro. And when I realized that there was a difference in the two systems, my son was doing in the third grade what they were doing in the first grade in Greensboro. So a lot of that had to do with—on my part—had to do with the school system. Now whether that was a good choice or a bad choice, I don't know. But he was, well, both of 'em were—the two older ones were—the oldest one was a smart child and my daughter was, too. . . . Well, she was diagnosed as dyslexic but I think a lot of that was poor preparation, so not necessarily true dyslexia, but just. Reflecting on the teachers, I was dissatisfied with the Perry County schools system as it was, so that you know, led to it some, and some of it was everybody following the crowd, too.

It wasn't an easy time to pull them out—for anybody—to pull children out of the public school system to put them into a private school, 'cause you had to do without.

What do you mean when you say that?

Well, 'cause, you had to pay for it.

Oh, you mean because of the expense of the private schools.

Uh huh—the expense was not something that—and now, those who stayed, and their kids did just as well as ours, but they still came out . . . a system that, like I said, I never was—I mean, after I realized the difference between what they were doing in one place as compared to Uniontown, I wasn't too happy with the school system, so—and it's easy to blame the school system for part of it, so . . . I'd hate to think all of it had been because . . . well . . . I think if it had been a good school system it'd have been worth something putting out the effort to keep them there. But, I don't think it was—and the grant wasn't in Greensboro—stayed good for many years. Now my brother taught there for years and years and years in the public school system—so I know it was a good system, but I'm not familiar with it now. I don't have anybody there, so—and haven't had for some time, but it's—

Really, that time frame is actually kind of a blur, because I don't have the memories of the boycotts and things that people around here did—that have been around here. It's just—I'm trying, I just cannot remember where people are now working. Must have been Uniontown but I was not. I was more or less insulated from what was going on in town, because if I remember correctly, I was probably working at the garment plant or somewhere—but anyway it was not in town itself, it was—if it was the garment plant it was just in a—

Do you mean if civil rights activity was in the garment plant?

No—that's where I was working and there wasn't any. That's why I'm having a hard time trying to figure out where I was at that time, 'cause my youngest child was born in '63, and I left uh, or, maybe I could have still been in Demopolis at the [inaudible] and . . . really . . . all I heard is secondhand. And that was how busy they were, and you'd hear things on television they expected this, that, and the other to happen that never happened in Uniontown. And, um, so I'm not really—I guess like I said, I was insulated from it all. I'm sure I worried about something happening and me being in one place and my children in another place, so that type of thing, but . . . I don't have a lot of memories about that, so I'm a poor one other than I'm different. I'm going to be mostly different from anyone else you talk with about it. Like I said, even the school system during the sixties itself all stayed put. I mean, we didn't—it was the seventies before we even—

Oh, before you desegregated—

Or went into a private educational system.

Did it desegregate before then?

Yeah—they were there. Blacks were in the school system not immediate, but it was early seventies before there were a lot, and before people started going in—before whites left for private school. So it was, and then there are not that many white children in Uniontown anymore, and hadn't been for years. A lot of the people moved to other areas. And like I said, the population itself is like ninety-nine to one right now. In fact, I doubt if there's a hundred white people living in the city limit. Well, in part of Uniontown. Well we have, Uniontown had a mill village, you know what I'm talking about?

A what village?

A mill village—it—years ago the economy was based on cotton and we had a—not even sure what they made in—the use of cotton. But it was a huge thing, and it had a village surrounding it . . . and a fairly large one. But we still have people who live. The cotton mill is no longer there. All you've got is a long slab of concrete that is huge—all that's actually left of the mill itself. But the houses are still there, but you've got some children out there, but not many. Most of those people with children have moved on.

So mill village—the mill was the center of the village? And people lived . . . were there merchants mostly around the village? Or were there residential homes?

Residential homes where the mill workers lived . . . and a lot of times the mills themselves built the houses for 'em—now I don't know whether—I'm sure they had to pay rent. I don't know how exactly that worked. I hadn't even thought about that part of it. But, you might've had a few stores, but most of the village itself was the homes for the workers in the mill. And that was, uh, one . . . two, three . . . streets—fairly long streets full of houses . . . and there are, like I said, there are still people out there with no mill, but they still would call it the village—it was the village.

And where were these located? Or, where was this one that you were talking about?

It was in Uniontown, now—at one time it was not part of the city limits—within the city limits, but it is today. And there's probably more whites out there today than it is in the town part—in the old town part where I live, but I'd still say the percentages are close to 99 to 1.

Okay . . . so what else would you say about your life? And I'm not specifically talking about race relations right now. How else would you describe your life in the fifties and sixties? Or just life in Uniontown?

Well—I guess—I think what developed is a lifelong interest in history, genealogy—and some of the things like that developed during that time period. Now why, I don't know. And my kids used to—my kids were traveling and . . . I had this box—just a stationery box. I usually just carry it with me, put my notes in, and my kids used to call it my cemetery box, 'cause we'd stop and visit cemeteries. But I grew up in Greensboro, which had a history—written history. And I came and moved to Uniontown and there was none. And I started, you know, just delving into history. And then from Uniontown it went to Perry County history and it just—and I've always loved genealogy. It's like a puzzle. Well, history is like a puzzle, 'cause I have a friend here on campus . . . we talk about our five hundred or five thousand mysteries we keep coming across. And we like to solve the mysteries of, and it's nice when you do find it's—or it's like a puzzle, putting it together, and you find that one piece, you thought you'd lost—it makes everything fit.

So what kinds of mysteries, just as an example? What's an example of a mystery that you're—

I was just thinking, I don't even think about it being a mystery unless Bill says something about it. We're working—well, the book's in publication. It's a pictorial history of Perry County—postcards and old pictures. And we've got a picture of a house from—we assume it's from here in Marion, 'cause it was in with a collection of other houses, but we can't identify it. Well, that's one of our mysteries. And then we found another one the other day that nobody seems to know. It's a picture of a house and it looks like its burning. And it was in the collection over at Marion Military Institute with some other Marion stuff, but nobody knows—not that house, so, you know—it's just those are our mysteries.

And I probably could think of others, but right off the bat those are the mysteries I'm referring to. I keep hoping that somebody's going to identify the house. It probably burned long ago, or either fell down.

Right . . . that's probably why no one recognizes it.

Yeah, well, it was a Victorian-type house but so many of the houses had burned over the years, so . . . but I, just . . . well . . . I just like to delve into the history. At least it can't haunt me. [laughter]

If you attack it head-on or at least if you face it head-on, it can't haunt you, right?

That's right. It's interesting—and it does help you to see the patterns why things are today as they are—makes me cringe when I think about what the children of today—that a lot of the schools don't teach a lot of the history that they used to.

What do you think is the difference between what they teach now versus what they taught then?

Well I don't really know, other than the fact that—well, and most of it's based on hearsay—but you see, so much of what's not in the history books anymore or they don't require this or that in the schools like geography—it's just, how can you really know where you are if you don't know where you came from?

And likewise, I like to know where these other countries are—what's going on in 'em. How many people knew where Afghanistan was? Or how many—if they—didn't know some. And it'd be awfully hard to understand some of the problems in those different areas if you didn't know the background on 'em. Look at Iraq. . . . It's a product of a lot of different—well, it's been around since biblical days. And you had problems then—and if you studied the history of it and knew something about it, you could understand why the different groups don't get along—and not just, that's besides the Americans getting involved in it—but the relationship between the different groups. If you hang out, and that's what a lot of people miss out on—is, you make snap decisions or snap judgments, and you may blame it on U.S. stepping in. But then after all, it could have been even worse 'cause those people didn't. They don't value each other, I don't think.

They don't what?

Value each other, cause they're—but, but that's just my—just think you need to know something about the world and what went on and what made us as we are today.

Reverend Richard Bryant

Rev. Richard Bryant, pastor of a Baptist church in Marion, Alabama, discusses civil rights activities in the 1950s and the 1960s, particularly some of the earliest activity involving a small and courageous group of men who organized in the 1950s, the impact that young people from the Lincoln School had on the Movement, and Jimmy Lee Jackson's shooting death in 1965. He also discusses some history regarding the Lincoln School itself, and offers many rich insights on the major events of the Movement from a spiritual perspective. Rev. Bryant also speaks to gender relationships and family within the black community in Marion then and now.

*Note: The first part of this interview took place in Marion standing just outside of Rev. Bryant's church in the presence of Ms. Frances Ford, director of Sowing Seeds of Hope, and Mayor Edward Daniel. Part II took place five months later inside the church sanctuary.

☐ ☐ ☐

Well, like I said, I was there [at Lincoln Normal High School] and graduated in '63. Things began to heat up . . . like Birmingham. We had some students, we classmates you know went to Birmingham, you know—when they had the riots up there. And then things just kept heatin' up, heatin' up, and heatin' up. So, by '65, you know, they was here then, start marching and, what not. And I always say that—you can't use this 'cause I'm gonna write a book on it.

I always considered this period of the incidents springing from Lincoln . . . what happened, you have students leaving Lincoln and went to town to march during school time. Matter of fact, most of 'em didn't even go to class that day. I always considered that as being . . . the spark that lit the fire. And that's the title of my book so don't write that. [Interviewer received permission later from Rev. Bryant to use this material.]

Some people say, now why would you say it was the spark that lit the fire? You have to understand that period of time when people were livin' on plantations and a lot of people was afraid of getting involved, and you arrest all of these students. Though we have a saying that you don't mess with black women's children, so a lot of 'em at that time wouldn't have got involved if they had not arrested those children. So then you got the black womens involved because then they have to find out where their children was—some were in cells in jail and in different places. So the women went, then that means the mens had to go. They forgot about whose place they was on and who they was workin' for and all of this . . . and then after that you had the Jimmy Lee Jackson incident, and then people got angry. As we say, they got mad. And it was no turning back. They just march—or meeting—mass meetings, they were there.

So I said with Lincoln, schools played a major part in the civil rights movement—because of that—those incidents, it just stirred people up, and that's really where the origination come from, or the civil rights march from Selma to Montgomery.

You have a lady by the name of Lucy Foster. After they killed Jimmy Lee Jackson, we already had the funeral, she suggested that we march the body from here to Montgomery and, you know, place the body on the capitol steps. But, you know, some of the leaders decided against that and said, no we'll go ahead and bury the body here and march from Selma to Montgomery. Lucy Foster was her name.

What years were you a student at Lincoln?

I graduated from Lincoln in '63—I was there . . . but I had brothers who was there at that time. You know, was at Lincoln at that time. But like I said, . . . most people just see "'65," But you have to remember there was a beginning. We had a few men around here who was even from the fifties, you know, was kinda trying to motivate people and get involved and they faith to believe that things were gonna change. . . . You know, I remember my daddy saying it was gonna happen. . . . But at that time it was kinda hard to see because, you know, other folk was in control. . . . You have to be in it—you have to live the period to really understand really what was goin' on, you know. When you talk about people was afraid, you know, wasn't so much that people was afraid, but, people had families, and nowhere to stay except on the plantation, and if they got involved in the Movement then this man would tell them to . . . you know . . . to move.

Was that your family's situation?

No it wasn't mine. . . . We was always somewhat independent you know, 'cause I really didn't never work for white folks. Course my daddy worked us to death. He was the boss. So we could . . . and people like my daddy, and other peoples you know, kinda independent but weren't stayin' on a plantation. They could afford to get out here and speak and talk and do things you know, and . . . the only thing they had to worry about was maybe the Klan or something like that, but as far as moving, that wasn't never a problem . . . but other folks, they couldn't, they couldn't do it . . . because like I said, they had to have somewhere to stay . . . and eventually, a lot of people did had to move off the plantation because of their involvement in the Movement, so you can understand. . . . You don't have anywhere to go! And if I get involved where am I going? If I get involved where am I goin' work? 'Cause all the work basically was on the plantation, you know, so it was just the situation. . . .

So that's why the children were so important to the Movement.

Exactly . . . because *they* could do it, but their mother was still at this side of the house, and Daddy was still working at Mr. Charlie's plantation. So the children could do it—and that's why they were so instrumental in using young folks. And then there's something about young folks anyway—they full of energy . . . half-crazy and fearless. That's why they were so important. Had it not been for using young folk it would have took much longer—to get it done. But like I said, all you know all you have to say young folk, let's go, and they're ready to go . . . They want go anyway.

I've been asking everybody what their remembrance was at the time—really, on the day Jimmy Lee Jackson was murdered.

Now that happened at night when he got shot. And they was having one of them normal mass meetings. Really to tell you the truth about it, James Orange was in jail—they had arrested him. He was one of the main leaders . . . he was leading everything. That night they had a mass meeting, and they were gonna leave the church and march right up the street to the jail. So when they come out of the church, and they kneel down to pray . . . by that time they had brought all state troopers from everywhere . . . and when they come out of the church, then they kneeled down to pray, and that's when they started beatin' them. Then a lot of people ran back to the church, a lot of people hadn't got out of the church, and really Jimmy Lee Jackson was down, right down the street in the back of the church, really just café he was in there that he was in then . . . they was beatin' his granddaddy, old man Cajun Lee . . . —that's how he got involved. They beatin' him—that's when they really shot him. But they intention was to march up to the jail, and, you know, maybe pray, and then go on back to the church.

Where were you that night? Do you remember?

Oh Lord, I was probably halfway across the world. No, I was in the military at that time. . . . My daddy, my mother, my brothers . . . all them were there . . . and we—uh, my daddy went for what we called church hogs, especially against white folks, where we teased him the rest of his life because that night, troopers and things was pushing folks in the Klan, or they guided him to his car but he left my mother. She ups there worried to death about him because he was always outspoken, you know . . . and we teased him about it . . . he went on home! And I think Albert Turner brought her home. And when she got there we laughed about it—we tell him he was at the house settin' to the fire—we had fireplaces then—he was at home settin' to the fire and not even going back to check on her . . . and she worried to death about him and then when she get home she find him in the house, settin' to the fire! [Laughter] But he claimed they made him get in his car . . . so he got in his car and he left! But we never did let him live that down, you know, that he left her—he was gettin' out of Marion so fast that he left her, you know! So he claimed he felt like she would be alright—they wasn't gonna bother her, you know. But he left and went on home.

But this place has a lot of history, you know.

I knew there was a lot of history here, but I didn't know just how much.

Yeah, but nobody pays that much—I still say if it had not been for those Lincoln students leaving school . . . See when they got to school that morning, James Orange was at the school . . . see and we used to drive just like outside the fence there [points to a fence] the bus would be lined up out there and you got off at the gate. So, my wife had me laughin'—had me laughin' about it—she said . . . her friend got off the bus and didn't go into campus and said, "Ain't gon' be no school today!" she said, um, she said, "How come?" she said, "Jesus said ain't gon be no school today!" and so she got off the bus and looked she said, "Where he at?" So they pointed at. James Orange—just outside . . . burly old black man . . . [laughter] it's like, he was Jesus! [Laughter] She said she told 'em, said, "Well, Momma sent me to school today, I better go to school!" [Laughter]

But a lot of the kids didn't go in—they just left then, but then a lot of them walked off the campus after that and . . . and they marched in town and they gon' go up here and marched in town . . . that's when they arrested her and put 'em in jail, and took 'em in buses and took some of 'em on back to Brent and put some of 'em in prison some of 'em in Selma, Tomilson, and so now you got . . . you got mothers, now! They're upset, and they don't know where they children are! Like I said, you don't make black women mad about they children!—and they didn't care what happens, no mo'! So from there on you had more and more people getting involved. You had more people from all over the county then, comin' up and, and meetin' at night you know, 'cause they were working in the day, but they was meetin' at night. And that's how you got so many people involved—and like I say, they got angry—and it was simply because of those children. If they had never arrested those children, I bet you 75 percent of those folk would have never gotten involved. And see, the . . . white folks didn't realize that, you know—they wouldn't a got involved in no movement! But it didn't matter how much they talked about "You're alright" and "We like you." . . . You couldn't tell them nothin' after that! You know, "I don't care what these white folk say. . . . You don't like me because what? 'They put my child in jail!'"

It was over then. It was over. You couldn't tell them nothing. You had some folks, like I said, they—I won't say so much afraid, but the condition and the circumstances . . . they just couldn't afford to get involved! And then we didn't have no houses for 'em . . . you know, so.

You didn't have what?

I said we didn't . . . black folks didn't have no houses for 'em, you know. If they got put off the place, or got put out of a house, we didn't have a house for 'em—where were they gonna stay? But like I say in the end they finally did . . . 'cause I know my daddy took one family, we had . . . bought a place then through the house-owners, so we let this family stay in that . . .

in that house—they're from across the river . . . so we let 'em use that house. . . . But anybody that had somewhere and they could help someone get in a house, they did.

So families were thrown off of the—

Oh yeah! You had to leave. Families had to leave! That's what I'm sayin' that's what made it so hard to get people involved because they didn't have nowhere to stay! You know, and if I get involved and you putting me off this place where I'm goin'? And like I said back in that time, mostly everybody was on a plantation—except a few folks living here in . . . within the city limits and I don't know—for some reason, it was easier to get people in the countryside involved than it was to get the folks in the city involved. A lot of folks just say, "I'm not gonna get involved in this."

Why do you think that was?

You have to understand the—I call it brainwash. It's something like . . . what it was . . . the priest or preacher in Germany . . . said they come and got the Jews and, ...so it was the same thing here. "They're not botherin' me," per se, which they were, but they didn't see it that way, so. . . . Until it affects . . . a lot of times until it affects you, you don't understand it, or you can't imagine what it's like. But my philosophy has always been if they do it to you, they'll do it to me. And eventually, most people find out that the same thing they would do to me they would do to them. You know, so they decide then. . . . What's you know, you ain't got no choice! 'Cause, eventually, they gonna get to me!

It's just like, in order to get you to understand it . . . say for example, Tiger Woods. He really didn't want to say he was black. He want to say he was mixed and all of this. But then, once he made a mistake then they let him know he was what? . . . [laughter] When he won the Masters they let him know he was what? [laughter] He was black!

Obama—wanted—Obama you look at all this talk they're doin' about he doing this he ain't doin' that—I mean, they got a nice way of putting it, but bottom line is, they consider him black! And that's what a lot of people have to realize sometimes, they say, "Well, he treat me alright," but I say if they ain't treatin' all of us alright . . . you ain't doin' nothing to treat *me* alright. As long as you treat *my people* wrong, then you treatin' *me* wrong.

It's just like biblical. In a sense. It's like Mordecai and Esther. Esther got to be queen . . . and she was alright! And Mordecai had to convince her that you still a Jew. And when they kill all of us, and they see you sittin' up in the palace, what you think they gon' do to you? And that's what's so hard sometimes to get people to understand. Is that . . . you black, you white, you Jew, and really it's just a stupidity, because all of us are the same. Everybody's blood runs red. But there will always be that feeling of racism. We so much . . . it ain't just them—we's racist too towards them—as much as they are towards us.

And it's all because of our lack of understanding, you know . . . and then you finally get into, I mean—it will always be to an extent—but we have to learn to . . . and what we trying to do now is—I use a pad up there to tell people this . . . that—all the birds share the forest. The turkeys, the ducks, the quails . . . and they can walk right through each other. But they don't forget— which bird they are when it becomes flocking time. I mean, they share the forest. And that's what we got to learn to do—share the forest. We have different cultures—we don't eat the same thing. We don't socialize the same way. But we all can get together and socialize. But when it comes flockin' time, we have to learn to flock together. You don't see turkeys trying to flocking with geeses! Geeses fly high and they fly in formation! Turkeys fly up and they scatter—they get back together once they land . . . maybe a block away! And so people have to be the same way. You can't wipe out a people's culture, but you have to get them to understand we have to live . . . together. And that forest belongs just as much to the turkey as it do the duck. And that's . . . that's what got us [inaudible] as a people . . . all over the world. Not just in America, but basically all over the world.

But I tell people all the time that this small town when you look at it—it rocked the world. This small town . . . when we start looking at history . . .

It's amazing when you really look at what happened here—nobody ever really pays it any attention.

Now Marion—the people in Marion, now they don't . . . people wonder why you can't just do 'em any kinda way. You got to understand that education plays—is the key—to any people. Marion—it had Lincoln school—it had an educational institute—so people got a little education, a little knowledge, a little understanding. Now as downplayed as this little town is . . . you can't come in here now, and act like you all that and we're . . . this town don't go for that. They don't think nobody don't know no more than they do, ain't nobody no more than they are. And I tell preachers when they come in. . . . You can't come in this town acting like you all of that trying to tell them what they don't know. Because really the history says that they are part of the cause that you . . . wherever you are and doing as well as you're doing. That's embedded in us. So, if you come to Marion . . . just . . . just blend in! If you don't you'll always be an outsider.

A lot of people come here and be at our church, and . . . but one thing, we haven't explored or motivated the people to understand the history of Marion and Perry County. Everybody . . . all the other cities like Birmingham, Selma, they get credit, they can get federal funds, all of this, you know, for their cities. Marion, they don't get anything. Now, one reason for that is it's somewhat—it has somewhat of a division among ourselves. Like I said, a house divided against itself can't stand. But if all of us get together on one accord, then we can let the people know what really happened here . . . get some recognition. I mean, some—a few people know—*we* know it, but . . . it's not public like Selma, like bridge crossing . . . half the folk down there are crossing the bridge from Perry County . . . you know. I bet it probably wasn't but 5 to 10 percent of the folk cross that bridge on Bloody Sunday was from Selma.

They were from Wilcox County, they were from Greene County. I'm telling you—75 to 85 percent of the people that walked across the bridge on Bloody Sunday was not from Selma. It really wasn't—like I said, the majority. . . I bet half of them was from Marion! They're from Marion. But you know, when you hear talk of it, it's like 70 is all. Like you said—half of them was on the porch looking!

[Laughter]

But I, you know, been saying I'm gonna write my book . . . and this past Christmas my daughter-in-law bought me a tape say if you're gonna write it, at least do some on tape. [laughter]

Frances Ford (FF): That's what we need, to start having so we can have it recorded because the history is so inadequately recorded because the people that actually recorded it are not the people that was . . . there. They wasn't here in Perry County. They weren't here in Perry County and they told it from that perspective. And many people that they have highlighted as heroes was really at home . . . they were at home and they came on the bandwagon later on.

Reverend Bryant: —no they didn't. See I'm talking 'bout the fifties when they started the bus boycott in Montgomery. Martin Luther King down there, they . . . organized what they called the . . . think it was the Improvement Association. And my daddy was a member. But, I can remember when, in the fifties, when they had folks like Cajun Lee, my daddy, James Howard, Reverend Walker . . . up this way [pointing up the street] . . . these mens in the fifties—now, it took—it took nerves, now, I don't say it didn't, . . . but they would gather up on in Marion on a Saturday and they would discuss these issues.

Everybody else was afraid! So you had, this what you call the *grassroots* . . . people, you know, . . . you had in the new men era you had people like James Avery, James Carter, folks like that—Luke Jackson—you know, but they were somewhat independent so they could afford to, you know, do it to an extent, uh, so they wasn't—

And then when, I tell people this . . . when Albert Turner came, it was like a Moses coming for these old men. They had the faith, they had the guts what we say, the "guts" to do it, but they were basically uneducated. So, here you got Albert coming along—he's young, he has been to college. And that's all they want, is somebody that had some education that knew how to do things that they didn't know how to do . . . they knew how to tell somebody how to do it but *they* didn't know and so that's why they just fell in behind him.

So this is the group of people you talked about including your father who would sit and—

See, they was already ready to go! And like I said, when Albert come along . . . it's like a Moses coming. You got a man that's young, plus he has been to college! You gotta understand now, see back in them times it was only so many people had a college education. It doesn't matter what field they was into—if they had been to college, these older folks could trust and believe that they know how to do it, but they was—they had your back. See, the old folks had Albert's back when he went out there . . . they didn't have to worry—if he said it, they were there. But it started from—it didn't start in the sixties, it started in the fifties. . . . Just these few men would get together and talk—

It was tough back then, see, I tell my kids a lotta times, when you talk about Bull Conner, I always wanted to know—I can remember when he was campaigning—park his bus at the courthouse, and he walk up and down the sidewalk and I was cross the street. . . . I was a teenager then and he was walking up and down the street, "We gonna get us some axe hounds and pig hound and we gon' beat all the Martin Luther King niggas down to the ground...."

I mean ... my kids .... they can't even imagine someone walking up and down the sidewalk talkin' 'bout they gon' beat niggas and this, you know, they feel like in this day and age you gonna' kill 'em—but wasn't nothin' we could do but listen! And that's what I did! I just stood cross the street there—matter of fact, most black folks didn't even take the time to even stand there and listen, ... but at least I had the nerve to stand there and listen ... at what he was saying—you know—that's hard to believe this day and age that that really happened in the fifties—see, and that wasn't no hundred years ago. I tell people all that stuff—this was like yesterday.

And now we done got up here now and think everything alright. It *still* ain't alright! But like I said—It ain't gon' change overnight. It'll be another hundred years, really, before things ... before you change a people from within. And that's what we're *trying* to do now. But it'll be another hundred years ... Some folks say, "That's a long time!" I say, "Yeah, it will be that long." We still, we don't want to admit it. ... But we still have that plantation mentality. It's in us!! When we ... if you watch people, you know, when white people start talking to 'em, and start talking nice to 'em—that's right now! I ain't talkin' about yesterday—that's right now. They start to laughing and, you know, want to be nice to 'em ... don't wanna ruffle 'em. That's right now! It's just in us! You have ten black people standing up here—and I could walk by, walk up—they might not hardly speak! White man walk up, "How you doing, Mr. John"—all of 'em! "How you doin'? How you doin'?" They don't realize, but it's still plantation mentality in many of us, and it will take another hundred years before we really feel like we're really equal. But—that ain't gonna happen overnight. But you don't stop working on it.

I always like to talk about leading up to the sixties. See, young folks [say]—I wouldn't a took that! I tell 'em all the time, your stomach will dictates what you'll take. I think it was Napoleon he say "army travels on this desert," you know. . . . So if you ain't got nowhere to stay and you ain't got no food, don't talk 'bout what you gon' take! [Laughter]

Thank you so much.

Part II: Interview with Reverend Richard Bryant

The fifties—in that transcript you will see where I said we was basically independent. My dad was raised somewhat independent by his father, and then he got in some trouble. And he did some time. And when he got out then he had to—he came worked for this—well, wasn't a plantation, but it had about five or six families on the place. So, he did that three years. Then after the three years we went back to, you know, independent. So . . . I had some experience on a plantation.

So when we talk about the fifties . . . everybody was farmers, sharecroppers . . . saw mill or whatever you wanna call it. But it was in the woods. So I mean, these were the only jobs. Basically anywhere between 75 to 85 percent black people working on the farm. I mean, that was just it. Either they was farming cotton, corn . . . there was somebody on someone's place raising cows. And then later on you had chicken, hogs. But it was basically farm work.

So, you didn't have many people, and again, I wouldn't say people was afraid or scared, but you have to look at the conditions and the circumstances. You had just a few black people that had their own places, and so due to the circumstances, there wasn't too many of them. Really wanted you to be on their place—they wouldn't have houses to put you in because they still have to deal with "the man."

So basically, everybody was living under those conditions. And when you talk about fear and all of that—and then the next thing you have to understand is that the law wasn't basically for us then, a few had a confrontation with a white man, who were you gonna call? The sheriff? He'd probably come out there and beat you to death. So you had to put up with it. And so all this was going on in the fifties. So you get in a rut, and you somewhat—you adapted to it. You lived with it. But still there is—in that basic organization that blacks always have had and still had, and which I say really is the only true organization that blacks really have is the church. I know all of you young folks don't know nothing about that.

But through the years, that's the only organization we had. And that's the only thing we could identify with. It's somewhat spiritual . . . sociable. When you got together socially, it was at church. Spiritually, it was at church. Boys saw the girls at the church. So, this was it.

So a lot of people wonder why the Movement really started—basically, all your meetings was at church. And that wasn't as easy as you think, now, because you still had somewhat plantation churches and you still had some preachers that wasn't gonna rock the boat, either. So they didn't—some of 'em didn't really want to get involved. And you might not believe it, but there was certain churches in the beginning that wouldn't host a mass meeting . . . because basically the preacher of that church may have been preaching to a plantation. Might have even been living on a plantation. So he was somewhat governed to what he could say . . . and, you know, and so he would say—well why would this be at church? But you still have that don't-rock-the-boat people. And you still have that today. Even in modern times. You still have people that don't want to rock the boat, you know. They want to stay in that comfort zone. They're complacent to stay right where they are. We're doing alright—just let it be, because things gonna remain the same.

I can remember in the fifties. Like I said, my daddy and 'em filled me in. We would talk about freedom, you know. And at that particular time it wasn't so much about voting. It was about having some freedom. Freedom to go and search souls. Freedom to go to restaurants. Freedom to go to certain motels. Freedom to, you know . . . just freedom. And you never realize how bad it was, because like I said, you become complacent. You accept things as they are. But the separate thing is going into a store, and you could be at the counter, with your merchandise on the counter, and they could be getting ready to add it up. And if a white man or a white woman walked up there, didn't nobody tell you to step back. This the way it was. You automatic. It was a psychological thing. You just step back because he felt like you supposed to. So you step back and [they] wait on them, and they start back to waiting on you. And if another white one come in, they stop before waiting on you.

This just the way it was. So when you come through that and you look back and a lot of people said things haven't changed. I can't say things haven't changed. There's a whole lot—it's the little things that we don't even take a second thought about. You know. And like I said, who can you go to? You had no black officials, no black lawyers, police all was white—where you goin'? Get yourself in some trouble, really. So we adapted to it. But through all of that, there was a spirit within—and when I say a spirit within you still had a few older folks that was quietly discussing and talking about it. And then you have to be there to see the doubt in the majority of the blacks because they were saying that things ain't gonna change. These white folks will always have it this way—they got all the power, they got this, they got that—there ain't nothing we'll ever be able to do about that.

And yet you had that faith—just a few of 'em was continually saying things gonna change. And like I said, the church was always that spiritual base, and when they was singing, you know—they did believe that God will provide, that God will make a way somehow . . . spiritually believe that there would be a change, that one day we would overcome. We would get there. But then, like I said, the majority just couldn't visualize that drastic a change.

And like I said we look at it today and sometimes we say well maybe if things hadn't changed—and in essence, they haven't. But the conditions are better, I'll put it that way. Because I'm a somewhat fond believer in the words of Solomon: the more things change, the more they remain the same. But the conditions have changed. I mean, I don't have any fear when I go in the store—if I'm first, I'm first. You know. If I go in a motel I don't have any fear that they're not going to accept me. So the conditions have changed. But basically, it's the inwards structure of all of us, black and white—and America from within—has really not changed. And what bothers me is the only way there can ever be a change is, and I don't mean just sitting around and waiting for God to hand you something. But he reveals things—when you think about a simple thing as repent. If you think deep you say, what's so important about that? And then you think about it—to repent means to admit. When I say to admit, that means you admitting you have a problem, I'm admitting I have a problem, and then we can do what? We can go about trying to solve the problem. That's what's wrong with America today. We won't admit we have a problem. You know as soon as somebody says something black or white, you know—if it's not politically correct, then, no I shouldn't have said that. It's there! And until you deal with it, it's gonna continue to be there. So when we look back at the fifties, sixties, even to this present time, the problem we still have is admitting we have a problem!

[*Some discussion between Rev. Bryant and me about this in modern contexts*]

And that's what really, from generation to generation, come from under bondage. Somebody decided that it's not worth it, and what do I have to lose? And that's what happened in the fifties. Some of 'em just said, well, what I got to lose? I don't have freedom now. What can they do to me any worse than they already doing to me?

But again, I say, if you weren't there it's just hard for you to visualize what happened during the fifties and sixties. Even for me, and I was there. Sometimes and I have to stop—that really happened? And really it was just yesterday. You talk about forty-fifty years. That's yesterday.

Sometimes I'm sitting down and watching documents, and I say, what? Have we taken in all of that? Yeah! We've taken all of it!

But then you have to—it's called survival. Black people have always been survivors. And when you destroy the family structure of any people, when you conquer the head of any people, you already have the people. Conquer. And I know in this modern society and women's liberation, they still say black men are all about nothin'. But when you look back through the history, that black man—he tough! First you gotta see in America he was brought here in chains—he was enslaved. Everything today was stacked against him. They put a division between him and his wife, between him and his children. He was a nobody, really. And yet, through all of that, what Langston Hughes says—and still he rise. What we've got to do as a people is respect one another and stop putting each other down. So really there is a war going on between black men and black women. It's a war. You might not realize it. And all that does is just bring us down. That ain't nothin' to hear a momma telling her children oh Dad ain't nothin'. And then that sinks into that child's head.

The man is already sayin' he ain't nothin'. So, then here the wife sayin' he ain't nothin'. Then the next thing you know the children sayin' he ain't nothin'. But if he goes down, the whole race goes down. I mean, these are basic facts, you know, but what we did have which kept us as well as it did was a family structure in the midst of trials and tribulation. It's the family structure that held us together, and our organization called the church. That's what brought us through the fifties. And there wasn't so much happening in Marion and Perry County.

Before you go to talk about that, can you say more about the family structure—was it just that families were intact, helping each other and supporting each other?

Yeah—when I said a family structure, you had a husband and wife and the wife basically supported her husband . . . and we talk about women's liberation, but black women always had to stand in front in a lot of instances, because she could say things and somewhat get away with it. But really a lot of times she had to speak for her husband. It was what he wanted to say, but she could say it and get away with it. But they were still together. And then families would help each other. If this family had twelve children and this family over here had one child or no children, their minds was always on their neighbor who had twelve children. And whenever they got something extra they would always give it to them and say here take this for them children. I mean, they was concerned. They said—if it was food or if it was clothes or whatever it was—take this for those children.

So you had a family structure not only in that house but in the neighborhood, so when we grew up, we think about the little things our neighbor did for us—words of encouragement they gave us. So when we went to school, we was concerned about making our neighbors proud, 'cause they was proud for us to succeed. And so that's what kept the families together. They helped one another—they provided for one another. They helped one another. They disciplined each other's children. You know, I would rather my neighbor to whoop me than for her to go tell my momma I was out of order over at her house. 'Cause you gonna get a killin', you know, it's because what they was saying then that you embarrassed them to where it's better that they whoop you and don't say nothin'. So, this kept families together. And that's why they wanted to know because if your child was doing something I was concerned about your child too, so I would tell you and so everybody just bonded even that whole neighborhood. But basically that's what kept everybody together because it really was just one family in a neighborhood. You know. In a church.

And when you get to school, I'm a firm believer in education—all an education is, is basically knowing how to provide for oneself. And I'm a stickler for education because you need it. I mean, God wants you to know. And he gives you divine wisdom to understand and do better. But not—I think sometimes we think in education, and educators do it, basically they think about an education—it's basically knowing how to make a fool of the uneducated. Yes, it's there. It happens. But that's not what education is about. And the reason I brought up education is because, when you said Marion, that's one thing that gave us some sense of hope. Some sense of pride, in that everybody had a little bit of education. 'Cause you had educational institutes. This is known as the Baptist Academy, ran by the black churches. They was interested in school. Most churches had schoolhouses at that church.

Even at that time in the fifties?

In the forties! In the thirties! They had school in the church. My home church we had a school and later years we had teachers in my time taught in those schools. And then we had Lincoln School. But see, really, Alabama State was really Lincoln Normal School, and it moved to Montgomery. So I'm showing you the importance of having an educational institute while everybody gets—all the students didn't graduate from Lincoln cause you know in my time or just before my time a twelfth-grade education was equivalent to a college education 'cause you had students that finished at Lincoln was aimin' to teach. But this was an educational institute. Then you had students—if they didn't have but two years to Lincoln and you had people out in the country—they would board in town just to go to school. So everybody had—you had more and more people who knew how to read. The scripture says my people will perish for lack of knowledge. So you had more people that had knowledge and spiritual wisdom. Because not only did you go to school, you went to church every Sunday, so you had the combination. So, an educated head with an uneducated heart—you in bad shape. What makes it work is the spiritual heart to absorb the educational head. Then it puts it to good use. And this is what I said brought us up through the ranks and through all the trials and tribulations and the turmoil in the sixties. Now we kind of like strayed away a little bit in the sixties 'cause we got what we call freedom and didn't know what freedom was.

In the sixties?

In the sixties. Oh yeah, we strayed away.

Strayed away in what way?

Spiritually. That's the only thing that destroys a people. Is when they stray away spiritually. Now I ain't the kind that every time I see you you talking about God bless you and I got a Bible under my arm. But it is the fundamental basis that God controls and he blesses you and he advances you according to how you honor and respect him. God ain't got nothin' against you having a Rolls Royce. He has two. But if you don't get it, he still demands the same respect, the same honor, the same glory. And if you do that, he'll take care of you. We at a standstill, really. I mean, we think we made all kind of advances but really we still in the wilderness. And the reason we still in the wilderness is because the bridge that brought us across was not our wisdom, not our education, not our money, not our power, 'cause we didn't have that. But it was God. And we done pushed him to the side. So therefore, we just wandering. When you disrespect God, then you disrespect your parents, then you disrespect your people. We in a situation now where we don't even have no regard for each other.

Now I know you all love to listen to what that name—hip hop and all them—and our children love to listen to that. Seriously that's degrading. But seeing all of this and seeing how we accept that, it tells us that we have drifted away from the base. And like I said, God don't care nothing about your owning a Rolls Royce or a mansion. It doesn't matter. All scripture is truth. And y'all don't know nothing 'bout Bible. Nebuchadnezzar was one of the first great kings—one you might consider a war ruler. But God made him a great king. And then, he was reminded of who made him this great king. And yet, one day walk into his palace and looking and talkin' about what a mighty building, what a mighty nation that I have. God gave it to him. But when he said that he had did it, then God let him know, okay—I'll take care of that. You gonna end up out there in that pasture with them cows, eating grass, dew gonna fall on you, I'm gonna take your little mind away from it, until you recognize that God is God. And that's what happened to him. And I was thinking last night, you know that's what we gotta do—we gotta stop and come back.

And God will carry us on farther but we done got to the point now where we think we did everything. Still thinking we did everything, you know. But when I look back through all of that, I can't see nothin' but God. When I look back even to—you know, my parents and my lifetime, where we were and to where we are today—I mean, just me personally, my granddaddy, he had a big store in between Marion and Uniontown, and he died, and so it was just my dad and his sister, and they just couldn't get along so he stepped out of it. And then you might say we started all over again—all this trouble he got into etcetera, and we came from.

My mother was a firm believer in education. My daddy, he believed you work, you know, so he didn't care too much about you going to school. Yet, he wanted you to be knowledgeable. But his thing was you work and do this and do that. And then you look at that, we struggled through that. Now don't get me wrong now. We had plenty of food 'cause he raised all that cows and hogs and all that. But when I look at how far we have come, and I'm talking about in my immediate family, you know, I look in, I'm trying to think, it's just one of us out of twelve, that graduate from college, now you know, I finished high school, went in the military, went to college for a while and that but just one. And yet when I look at all of my five kids, they had to go to college. You know, if you don't stay but a day you gotta go. But then when I looked and I see and I come to the building sometimes and I see my son walking down the street with his phone in his hand—he goin' to the courthouse to defend somebody, and then I look back to fifties and sixties. This was unheard of. So I have to say thank you, Jesus.

When I see some of my neighbor's children, sitting at a desk, the head of this and head of that. I say thank you, Jesus. No we haven't got where we should be, but we'll get there. But we gotta come back to the foundation. See a lotta time we blame the man. You ain't got to worry about the man. You keep the man in the other man's hand. And he will guide you to where you're supposed to go, once you let head and heart work together. And we done got top-heavy as a people because we dealing strictly now with head. Ain't no heart no more. And I'm not talking about everybody. But as a whole, we're top heavy because we're not concerned about anybody but us—you know, ourselves. And I tell people all the time, when you talk about where God has brought us from through the fifties and sixties and up until now, our problem is selfishness. Selfishness. 'Cause we teach our children go to school, get yourself an education, get yourself a good job, where you can have it made. And say that's not nobody else's business.

So you can have a house. You can have a big house. You can have a nice car.

But there is nothing in there saying that you might help somebody.

And yet the scripture is really clear about that.

And I teach 'em that in the church all the time. I tell 'em, people are money. And we don't think about people—we don't think about nobody but ourselves. If you think about people, you got money. If I think about making something for people, I'm thinking about people. They need, or they're going to want it. Therefore they're going to buy it. That's money. I don't have to think about me if I think about you. If I think about you might want some shoes, I'll make some shoes. When you think about Campbell soup, that man was thinking about poor folk, wasn't he? He didn't make it for dogs!

But in doing that, it was money. And that's what we have to get our people to realize. You don't have to depend on nobody else. Trust God, depend on him, and depend on each other. And you can rise—what—we're not a rich people. But if we were to unite, we'd be tough. But the key to it all is divide and conquer. And I have to give the man credit. He done a heck of a job.

And you know I tell people you know you all go to church and pay your dollar and your offerings and your answer is right there in your faith because you don't pay it any attention. I say, it ain't about shoutin' and getting all emotional. It's about truth. And Jesus said a house divided against itself can't stand. He can't be a liar. And they believe that. And they use that. And it works. It's still working. That's why I said it's nothing new. The more things change, the more they remain the same. It's the same old thing, over and over again. What the man name come over here and taught 'em how to master slavery—William Lynch. That's all his philosophy was; divide and conquer 'em. Put fear in 'em. And it's still workin'. And we don't stay close enough to God for him to open the wonders and let us see that this is what causing you your problems. Unity is strength. If you put all your money together and go to the bank and say okay we want a hundred thousand dollars, how the banker keep— banker can't refuse. But you can have a million dollars up there in that bank. And you don't want me to have a hundred thousand. So you don't have to say nothing to the man about letting me have cause you wanna be a top dog.

And that's what kills us, and that's what's holding us down from the accomplishments we made in the sixties. That's why we at a standstill. And we gotta teach our children that it ain't over. And you don't teach 'em hate. I don't teach my children hate. I tell 'em you got to love white, black—all of us the same because when you become totally educated, spiritually and physically, what's the difference between me and a white man? It's the stupidity of saying that causes us to be in all of this drama. His blood runs red just like mine. We're all the same.

But then you ask me how long will it be before it gets to the point where everybody will accept everybody, and my answer is when you see Jesus ascending down out of heaven, it will all be over. Until then, that will be the vision, because your archenemy is still here teaching, preaching division. And we ain't goin' nowhere as long as that happens. But y'all don't understand when we here again, the same. We come a long ways, but we have a long ways to go. Like I said, the little simple things that you all take for granted is so important. Such a great price was paid. We had to beg to go to the polls and vote. Now we're the most forgiving people, but we're so quick to forget. And then we use that on the Bible—God said he'll cast your sins into the sea of forgetfulness and remember them no more. And when they start out—okay if that be true, he don't hold that against you but physically forgetting and mentally forgetting that is not what it means. Because as often as Israel sinned against God and turned against God, what did he say? He brought you out of—

Slavery in Egypt.

If that be the case neither guy would bring it up. . . . But we're so quick to want to forget. Even blacks, you know, sometimes we talking about what happened in the sixties—all that stuff was in the past, I don't wanna talk about it. It just makes me mad. I say you need to hear it every day to remind you where you come from, who it were who brought you where you are. . .

And I tell 'em we're that close to slavery and don't know it. Because God has fixed it where we can vote, what we fought for—it's just like readin'. Y'all hate to read. And it's sure 'nuff bad now cause y'all got computers.

And I tell young folks all the time I say anything you wants to know is in a book. It's already been written down. If you wanna know you gotta look in this book! We don't want to do that. And that's another thing that's holding us back. And then we don't want to think about reasons for things. I was teaching them Sunday school on Sunday and I was saying that the reasons, 'cause I was trying to get 'em to understand why we go down to Selma and why we go across the bridge—what it symbolizes. It's important not to forget it. I say just like the Passover, when God passed over the Israelites and Israel. I said then in Jesus time when it came time for the Passover, they didn't ask him, Master are we gonna celebrate the Passover? They say, where do you want us to prepare for the Passover tonight? Just that important. And Jesus told them what to do, where to go and come certain man and I said that's all this is.

It ain't all about us glorifying ourselves. It's something that we should never forget. The meaning of this bridge crossing. If it were not for that then we wouldn't have a voting right act. It ain't about us just walkin' cross the bridge but it's to remind us that God one day delivered us. That he allowed us, through this act, that a voting right bill would be passed, that we might have the right to vote and speak up for ourselves. Vote for ourselves. That he did that for us. And we lost that. And until we go back there, we're gonna continue to go down—oh God gonna continue to hold us in his hand. But what's the use in taking such a beating when all you have to do is straighten up? You know the other folks are against you. I mean they continue to do it. You already know that. What you keep beatin' up on yourself for?

When the [inaudible] all you have to do is turn back and start back when, like we say, helping one another and loving one another and that's how people raised twelve children and that's all gotta do now. We know. It's in us. But, when the head becomes greater than the heart . . . and that's where we are now. And that's where we are now. Our heart has left us. 'Cause we don't care about one another. When I say that I don't mean everybody. But as a whole—as a people, we are too concerned now about self, partying. I hear people—I know everybody look at me crazy when I say this—that we said it's a curse now. Really. Among us as people. For somebody to have more than one child. When you think about—what you come here for. I mean, think about it there. You can accomplish what you want to accomplish. But if you haven't done anything to manage it, really you're living in vain. You know, and that's something else we done got away from. They done trained y'all well. Get yourself a good job. And don't marry that old no-good man.

They say don't marry a no-good man?

That's what they be saying now. Don't have no children now. When you have one you cursed. Don't have no children. If you have over one, you cursed. When the basic fundamental facts is children are a blessing from God. So you gonna turn down a blessing from God and accept a blessing from Satan. Think about it. And it's hard to swallow in this modern society. But when your head is educated and your heart is not educated you can't understand it. And that's why we can't understand what's happening to us. I tell people all the time. My wife, before we got married she said, I don't know if I wanna have children. And I said, well, I wanna have children. So she decided, well I guess if he want 'em then I guess we'll have 'em. And, um, we had five children. And the only thing I asked God was I wanted one daughter, and I ain't have no limit on boys. He gave me a daughter first, and then he gave me four boys.

Why did you only want one daughter?

I guess it was somewhat selfish. I didn't want to have to be chasing boys like they chased me. [laugher]. Keep me from reapin'! [laughter]

So the Lord blessed me and he gave me that one and he gave me four boys. And the amazing thing about it is she never wanted a sister. Not 'til this date. She gone and got grandchildren.

[*Chatter about his daughter ensues for several minutes*]

But just looking back to where I come from in a short period of time. When you talk about forty, fifty, or sixty years, that ain't no time. But it shows you where God has brought us from and we should be grateful and thankful. That don't mean go home and sit down, there is still work to be done; there's fighting to go on. But we've got to come back—we've got to come back together. That's how we made it over—that's how the voting right—like I often tell you about Lincoln is when you stood up for people—something they care about. And arresting children and putting them in jail—something we cared about. So therefore, everybody rose up. Everybody got together—even the people who sat back and say, I'm not going to get involved with this mess. When they raised their children—and you know when you're young, you're foolish anyway. So if my friend going to get involved in it, I'm going to get involved in it. And that wasn't easy because at that time, when your parents sent you somewhere, they meant for you to do just that unless you went back and got permission.

Now you gotta understand this is in the sixties; these children are at school—you got James Orange and them standing on the other side of the fence, you got James Orange as they got off the bus, telling them, ain't gonna be no school, and they passing the word down—some of 'em say Jesus said there ain't gonna be no school. But they momma done sent them to school. And normally, you did what them folks said. But a lot of 'em didn't. And you know, when my wife was living she used to say, well them folks, she got off the bus and some of her friends rode the bus with her, stepped off said, ah, you goin' to school today? She said yeah. They just stepped off the bus now. And her friends said, well, Jesus said there ain't gonna be no school today. So she said who is Jesus? And so they pointed and saw James Orange—this big ol' black man. [laughter] She said well if my momma sent me to school I'm going to school! [laughter]

So, you had this inwardness in most of those children that some of 'em didn't go on the campus and others walked off the campus. And went on to town and got involved in the march. And then they got arrested. So those people—I mean, God works in mysterious ways. So those people who was hell bent about not getting involved, I thought Mr. Charlie was pretty good to us, and they wasn't gonna get involved. But when they saw Mr. Charlie go and arrest my child, just like he arrested your child, it's time for us to get involved. And that's what they did. They got involved. And they just kept going and kept going and kept going. People were angry.

I mean, Jonah got angry because God sent a shield, and then God said it does you good to be angry. Because it reminds you that if you got that much compassion for just us and here are a whole city of people down here and we don't care whether they perish or not. So sometimes it does us good to be angry. Makes us think. That did us good to be angry then because it made us—let us see that you needed mercy just like I need. You need compassion just like I needed compassion. It brought us together. And sometime I say we need to have films or sit down and talk to our young folks every week. At least spend five minutes in Sunday school, talking about what God has done for us, where we come from, where we had hardships, but then God still took care of us. And show us that sense of independence. I tell people today the last thing I worry about is eating as long as God reigns, and there's green vegetation.

That's just the last thing I worry about. And they say well why? And I say because I was basically raised on wild game—that's meat—and I look out there and I see rabbits jumping around in the yard, squirrels jumping around in the trees, deer running through the woods. If I sit around and starve, that's my fault. I don't consider that a hardship. Ain't no chicken in the store, when there's meat running round right in my face there—all I gotta do is get it. God has provided and a lotta times we complain to God and he's provided and providing. 'Cause we got children now they have gone to every major university in America and are going. But are they bringing those resources back to their community? No.

'Cause the higher y'all get up, the further y'all want to get from your neighborhood.

If they clean off those woods back there and build million-dollar homes and call that a certain neighborhood and everybody go flocking there. That's round where the ghetto at. Clean it up. Fix it up. When you get rich, be in your house in that neighborhood and make everyone else come up to par. They don't have to build a million-dollar house, but they can build a nice house. They can keep the yard clean. They can do all these things for themselves as they do for others. You know, but we in trouble but not from the outside—we in trouble from the inside out. That's what killed us. As they say, it's us that killin' us. Because we don't see what's happening. I don't care what kind of neighborhood them other folks building out here. You don't have to tell me to come—you don't want me in there. You don't want me in there and I don't wanna come in there. I don't want you around me either. I don't want you around me—I want to get as far away—personally I don't want nobody jammed up under me. Black or white. So why am I gonna go running under—you don't want me over there.

And I don't want you to tell me I can't if it's a public place. But I don't want to be with you no more than you don't want to be with me. Two months ago—three months ago they called us to have a unity meeting down here in Marion, and I went, and somehow or another they went round to everybody. I was the last somebody they got to, and so I said well, I'm all for unity. Unity is strength. I'm a firm believer in it. And you know, we talk about integration. I said, but how many of y'all houses I been to? How many of y'all been to my house? How many of y'all been to my church? How many times you see me at your church? I says it ain't all about that. I said the question—what the issue is about is, are we gonna deal on an equal basis? Or do I have to come to the table, sit down prepared to give up 80 percent, and you give up 20 percent. Now if that's the way you thinkin', as much as I love you today and I believe in unity, I just as soon to keep fighting!

Because that's not real unity.

Uh-uh! Just in the name of—and that's what got America in trouble. Everything we do is just in the name. We're not sincere about it. Every time you look it's something wrong. And we're in the name. And like I said, even the church wanna be politically correct. Eh. Let's be politically right sometimes. [laughter]

[A conversation about politics ensues]

You can put on the record I love white folks. I say I love 'em. But I don't have to like what they do. And I don't like a lot of things they do. And I wouldn't have it no other way. I wouldn't live anywhere else in America, except Marion, Alabama. New York, Washington, wherever y'all named. I'd rather deal here with these folks here. I think that much of Perry County, I think that much of my people, I think that much of all the people in Perry County, black and white.

They call me some kind of political—but I'm not political, really. I'm more spiritual than they think—than most preachers are. 'Cause in the final analysis, I'm always pointing to God. He's superior. He is the one that leads us, guides us, motivates us. And whatever happens I'm always pointing you back to He's the one that did this. He motivated us to do that. It's like I tell 'em. I don't want you praying to God to send me some bread and it's already in your kitchen. You can't pray for me with the bread in your kitchen. Give me the bread. And then both of us can pray and thank God for what He has done for both of us.

I can't hear your prayers only—feed me! And then tell me what God has done. And I can see the works of God because he already blessed me. And I can tell people God can give one person ten people's blessings. Ten. But you share it and spread it out and it makes it better for all of us.

I mean, you know there are some involved in what we call politics. In what we call civil rights. But it all boils down to that simple, basic, fundamental fact. The truth that Jesus said. Love ye one another as I have loved you. Unconditionally.

Evelyn Turner

Evelyn Turner, wife of former civil rights leader Albert Turner Sr., discusses the culture and customs in Marion during her childhood and teenage years as well as civil rights activity in the 1950s and '60s, including secret organizing meetings in the 1950s. She discusses her time as a student at the Lincoln Normal School, Jimmy Lee Jackson's death, the march from Selma to Montgomery, and the battle for voter registration rights. She also discusses political successes for blacks in Marion during the 1970s and the "trial of the century" in the 1980s involving the Turners and accusations of voter registration fraud.

☐ ☐ ☐

Did you grow up in Marion?

Yes.

So you were born and raised here—have you lived anywhere else?

No—only in the summer I used to go to Gadsden to stay with my mom 'cause my grandmother raised me and my brother and a cousin.

You met your husband here also?

Yes.

And he was born and raised here?

Yes, he was born and raised here and we met one Saturday by midday. I was walking the town from right down the road there [pointing outside]. I was walking to town and so he stopped and asked me did I want a ride. And I looked over and see who it was and it was him and I knew him from school, you know. And I told him "yes." And he said, "Well, what are you doing walking?" And I said, "Well we don't have a car, so you either go in the wagon, or you walk." And so he picked me up and he went into town, and I went on and did what I had to do and I reckon he did what he had to do. And that Sunday evening we were all sitting at the house and I saw this red and black Pontiac coming down the road, and I thought it was my uncle because at that time he had a red and black Pontiac. And I just ran in the house and I told my grandmomma—I said, "Here come Uncle Shipp!" That's what I said. And she said, "Oh—Shipp comin'?" I said, "Yeah—here come his car down the road now!" So when he got here, I said, "That ain't no Uncle Shipp!! That's Mister Turner!" [laughter]

Well, he came down to the house, and we started talking, and then one thing led from one to another, and then he came back and saw me . . . 'cause back in the day you never—you didn't receive company but twice a week, and that's on Sundays and Wednesday night—the boy could come see you, but he had to leave at nine o'clock! [laughter]

Yeah, he had to come in the daytime. And at nine o'clock he had to be getting outta there—whether he had a ride or not, he had to! [laughter] So, um, he came back that Wednesday night and we sat there in the living room and we talked. And then, when 9 o'clock, my grandmother says, "Ahem!" He said, "What's wrong with Gran?" He called her "Gran." I said, "It's time for you to go! You don't want her to start beating the pan!" We just laughed it off. And so I walked him to the door and he left. And then the next Sunday night he came back, and he asked me if I wanted to go to BTU—that was [a] program at the church that he was going to—his church. They had to go to BTU every Sunday night. And he had to—they didn't have but one car, so he had to go pick up his parents and the children . . . and I think it was about five of them, and they all piled up in the back seat, and the momma, the daddy, all of 'em got in the car. I told them, I said, "Well, there's no room for me!" He said, "Oh you could just sit close up under me!" [laughter] So we went onto church.

What's BTU?

That's an organization—a Baptist training organization at church. You'd learn about the Bible—my husband was the Bible teacher, so he would have them learning the books of the Bible—you had to learn them by heart and tell where they are found, you know. He'll call out certain scriptures and then you had to remember what scripture whether it was in the Old or the New Testament, and that's what they would do.

So he did that even before you were married and after you were married?

Mmm-hmmm. We got married in '57—December . . . Oh God I done forgot the date. The ninth—I had to think about it. December the 9th of '57. That's when we got married. But we didn't have no big old fancy wedding like they have now. We just went to the courthouse and we got married. And we stayed together for forty-three years and then he passed.

We got married, and then, he had to go to work—he was working in Tennessee—he was a bricklayer and he was working up there. So I stayed here in Marion. And then he took me up to my mom's and I stayed up there. She lived in Gadsden, so I'd stay up there with her until the weekend then we would come here.

And we did that until we got a house . . . with three rooms—a kitchen, bedroom, and a front room. And we thought we were . . . living good. It didn't have a inside toilet. So it had the outside toilet, and I was scared to go out there because I had never gone to no outside toilet. [Laughter]

And so going back a little bit further, what were your parents' occupations?

They were farmers.

Did you have siblings?

Yes, I had a sister next to me, but she died when she was a baby, and my brother. So it was just the two of us—my brother and I. And then I had a cousin—my mom's sister had a child, and she grew up with us. So it was three grandchildren living in the house with my grandmother.

And look like we had to walk fifteen miles up the road to catch the bus, but these kids can walk right out the house into the bus, and still the bus got to wait on 'em!

We had an old bus—forty-six—that was the number—and we could hear that bus coming 'bout five miles . . . and we were running trying to get to the road before he got there, 'cause if you weren't at the road . . . The only somebody that he would wait on was my cousin 'cause she had polio when she was young, and she was crippled and she had to wear a brace on her leg. Now he would wait on her, but he wouldn't wait on nobody else . . . ooooooh! We had to run, run, run . . . then when you get to the bus you saw . . .

We had to walk every day. And if you got left, bus left, you'd go back home, my grandmomma would make you pick worms off the greens, or wash quilts, or do something. You wasn't gon' play, you wasn't gon' sleep. You would be working the whole time 'til 3 o'clock. And then it'd be time when we got out of school. . . . We'd go in the house and we'd eat a little something, she'd probably had some baked sweet potatoes and you got a glass of buttermilk. And you had that, and then do your evening chores, getting in wood, until time to milk the cows, then we had to milk the cows. . . .

That's a lot of work!

Oooohhhh! Then we had to come in the house and get our lesson. And at that time we didn't have no electric lights, we had kerosene lamps. And you had to hurry up and get your lesson before it got too dark because you had to get lessons up and get bathed up. . . . You had to heat your water on the stove, to take a bath in those big tin tubs. . . . It was a mess.

But we did it. And I was on the honor roll. My ninth year in school I stayed on the honor roll, 'cause I had to get my lesson. 'Cause there was a girl that lived behind us, way down in the woods, behind us. And grandmother used to tell me—"If Ethel Ann can get on the honor roll you can get on there, too!"

And honey, I had to study my lessons so I could get on the honor roll so she wouldn't be fussin'!

I graduated from Lincoln. My mother wanted us to come to Gadsden my eleventh grade. Was it the tenth grade? Yeah, tenth grade, I went to school in Gadsden, but I didn't like it. So the next year, I came back . . . but you know the country schools were ahead of the city . . . the schools up there. 'Cause the story that Ira quoted on we had had it a year before—the Rabens? And, uh, I made that report and got an A+. And she asked me what school did I go to and I told her Lincoln Normal—that's the name at the time—Lincoln Normal High School . . . and she said, "Oooh, you went to Lincoln? That's the best school in the state of Alabama!" And we thought oooh we were doing something. And so I finished that year, the tenth grade there, and my eleventh year I came back here and went to school here my eleventh and twelfth grade and graduated.

Albert graduated a year before. . . . No, he had graduated three years before I did. And then in 1953 he graduated from Alabama A&M, and he came back. . . . I was in the twelfth grade then.

Did you go to college, too?

One year. I just went down to Wallace. It's in Selma. . . . Oh I had married then, and had all my children. And I went down there . . . because after I finished school I got pregnant [laughter] and then I had that one child, and then a year and eleven months I had another one . . . and three years, I had a miscarriage, after my daughter, and the third year, here come Wayne, the nurse . . . and then I thought I was through then, and here come little Albert. [Laughter] I said, "Well, this is it!" . . . three boys and one girl.

I would love to hear what it was like to be at Lincoln Normal School.

Oooooh, honey! It was the bomb! But you got your lessons! They didn't play! And if the teacher gave you an assignment, you got it . . . and if you didn't bring it in, you just go on stand up in line, 'cause she was gonna give you a paddling. Yes, you was gon' get a paddlin' if you didn't get that homework. So you knew!

My brother was in another section of the eighth grade. . . . They had so many sections. We graduated from Marion public school. They had first to the sixth grade . . . and then after then, you go over to Lincoln for the seventh through the twelfth. That was all black

Where did the white kids go to school?

They went to Marion Seminary. . . . It's over there by the Board of Education. . . . That was their school that is falling down now. That was their school. The elementary was on one side of the street and the high school was on the other.

My kids was the first blacks to go to the elementary school. . . . Spencer Hogue's children, Pat Davis's children . . . and Nate

Sullivan's, but mine's was the first. . . . There were just three families that went there to integrate it . . . and the next year got more, and more went over there. Let's see . . . it was in the sixties. 'Cause that was jus ... 'bout '64 or '65 . . . uh-huh . . . right in there. . . . '63, '64.

So that's how Lincoln Normal produced such good students, 'cause they were serious about everyone doing work, getting work done. And do you remember who the principal was at the time?

Mr. Fincher. Charles Fincher.

I heard about a lady . . . I'm not sure she's the person who founded Lincoln Normal School—was it a woman?

Mmm-hmm—yeah. 'Cause my aunt and my grandmother started there. She didn't graduate. She went to school there . . . mmm-hmm . . . All of my family went there.

Last time I was here, you were telling me a little bit about some of the organizing that had taken place in the late fifties—the civil rights organizing.

Mmm-hmmm . . . They met out in the woods . . . at a place called the Sportsman Club. That's where they used to meet out there. And that's how they got organized.

And do you know what sparked those meetings? Was it just discontentment?

Well, no—a lot of people hadn't gotten registered—didn't have anyone hardly registered. Blacks—I think they said they had about 150 blacks on roll that could register to vote, and then if you went up there to get registered, you had to carry one of those guys up there to verify that you were the person that you said you were . . . 'cause I know a lot of them went up . . . and Mr. Jim Webb . . . he owned a lot of property at the time and he would verify a lot of people. Jim Webb, Mr. Goree, James Goree, Palmer Goree . . .

And these people—was it just because they owned a lot of property that made them able to—

—and they had business . . . 'cause Mr. Webb owned a café, a barber shop, and a beer joint, and then he had a lot of houses that he rented, too. He had a lot of real estate. That's what we call it now—back then he just owned a lot of houses that they could rent to people. And Goree was a bricklayer. He laid a lot of brick for whites . . . didn't many black people had brick houses—Jim Webb had one. I think he was the first brick house . . . and then Mr. Goree finally bricked his own house . . . and who else had a brick house then? James Goree didn't have one, he had a brick veneer—the brick just came up to his window.

So, these were blacks with businesses and houses.

Mmm-hmmm. Now Mr. James Goree—see, there were two Gorees: one was a bricklayer, and one was a painter, and he and his dad used to do a lot of painting. But the old man Goree had all the white businesses, painting for them, and his son took it up for him when he died.

What was it that sparked all these meetings? It was the whole fight to register?

Well, Albert came back . . . and when he went up there to get registered they wouldn't let him get registered. He had to go get Jim Webb or somebody to vouch for him. And he said he wasn't doing it. He was man enough—he had gone off to college he got his B.S. degree and came back, and couldn't even register, so that's what sparked it. People couldn't get registered to vote. And so they wrote letters to the federal government. I had a lot of those letters, but they got burned up. Yep, they set my house on fire in '85. So all that history got burned up. We didn't know to go get a vault or something, you know, to put that kind of stuff in.

So your husband started these meetings—how did he decide who to call together?

Well, people who was dissatisfied with what was going on—they came to the meeting, people from the North, from all sections of the county except Uniontown. They never would have anything to do with the Movement because they said that they were doing fine with their white folk. They didn't have—Well, if you would go to Uniontown . . . not so much now, but back in the days, everybody was half-white.

The white folks would go with the blacks—Alberta Goree—all of those folks that was down there, they are white—half-white—they have one parent that is white. And, like Viola's mom, didn't even allow her children to play with blacks. And she kinda funny now! [soft chuckles] She just started associating with blacks. She wouldn't let certain people come to her house.

What happened in Uniontown?

They just like day and night from Marion, 'cause I worked at the district judge office for eight years, and a man who owned property in Uniontown, he had the washhouse, they call it. And he came upstairs one day to my office. And he said, "Ms. Turner, why is Uniontown so different than Marion?" I said, "Well, more people in Marion have PhDs than the state of Ohio—" But . . . he said, "You know, that is true. . . . You all are more educated than those folks down there." I said, "Yes." But I don't reckon they saw the need to go to school. Something—I don't know what's wrong with them—

And he said he had a washhouse down there, and he said, "Ms. Turner, they do everything down there at the washhouses but wash." I said, "Really?" He said, "Yes . . . you can come in there go in there, look in the washing machine or dryer. . . ." He said,

"I have to get someone in there to clean them out!" I said, "You got to be kiddin'." He said, "No, I'm not, you can go down there any day . . . and that's what you will find, in his washhouse." He said, "I'm trying to make it convenient for people that do not have washers from home." They can come there and do their washin.' But, that's what you'll find—I couldn't believe it. . . .

That says they don't have no education. . . . They don't have any self-esteem.

No self-respect whatsoever. You find a juke joint on every corner. You can go down there now, and you can tell where they are because there's no whites—the whites have moved out on the outskirts—those that had moved to Demopolis, 'cause Demopolis is right down the road.

. . . Back then, it was horrible. They [blacks] just sold whiskey on every corner. You could just get you some Joe Lewis anywhere down there—that's what they did.

So, having the Lincoln Normal School, would you say that was the key part of—

Oh yes! That was the whole key. . . . 'Cause you had self-esteem, you had respect for others. And the elderlies? You just didn't talk any kinda way 'cause back then if your parent wasn't around, your grandparents were, and if Miss Susie says she saw you doing something you didn't have no business doing, she will whip you, and then when you got home, you got another whipping, so everybody took care of everybody children. You just didn't do no anything! And like these kids walk around with their pants hanging down . . . ooooh! You would not have gone that way, honey—not back in the fifties nor the sixties, cause those teachers really cared 'bout those children—they didn't live at home, they had a teacher dormitory and the teachers lived in the dormitory and they would go home to their families on the weekends. Most of them didn't have children—their children were grown or something. And those were the type of teachers that would come in.

Where were the teachers coming from?

Everywhere. Oh they thought it was just great to teach at the Lincoln School.

Any white teachers?

Not when I was going. It was sorta like a Catholic school back in the days . . . 'cause the lady that founded it was a missionary, and they had nuns teaching there then. But when they sold it [to the Board of Education] then that's when the nuns stopped taking care of the school.

And the board was run by white people?

Whites . . . whites only—no blacks.

Do you know anything about how they regarded the school?

Well, we always got books that came from the white school. But we used those books. You didn't leave those books at school. You carried your books home and you studied out of them. If your page was missing, you'd borrow somebody's book, or you copied what you needed to copy and get your lesson. We didn't get brand-new books—we just got used books. And we used the ones that was good and the ones that weren't good. But we got our lesson.

How do you remember your teachers handling cultural history? I would imagine that the textbooks that you were getting from white schools were either degrading or just didn't say anything about black history. Do you remember how you dealt with it?

We just dealt with it as they saw it. They did their teaching, and you had to learn, if you want to make it in this world, you have got to have an education. You will not make it if you don't have an education. You'd just be throwed away. They would tell you that, and you just didn't want to be thrown away. You wanted to be somebody. You wanted to take part in what was going on. So you just learn all you could!

They [the teachers] used the textbook, but they always learned—taught you, the facts of life—'cause a lot of them weren't used to what was going on in the country, in Perry County—that wasn't going on at the time. So then they would tell you, and the children would in turn tell them about what was going on. They will teach you about Europe and those other countries—what was in the textbooks. But then they also taught you the facts of life. 'Cause we had a teacher that was named Miss Lock. She was the math teacher, and we had a teacher named Mr. Jefferson. And he was the history teacher. And we had one named Ms. Perry—she was the English teacher. She told you about the birds and stuff like that. And then we had a science teacher, Mr. Cansada. He was the lab teacher. I can kinda remember you know, 'cause we just had our fiftieth class reunion. And well, my brother was always talking about Ms. Lock 'cause she was up teaching one day and he was looking out the window, and [he] said she came back there and "bap, bap—bap—bap!! Turn around! Your mind's supposed to be in here, not out there! You just wait 'til I see your grandmomma!" My brother said he never will forget that. So he never looked out there. . . .

So I'm interested in hearing more about the meetings that were taking place at the Sportsman's Club.

Well, they met out there for quite a while, 'til I think it's about '65, then they came to town, and they started to meeting at the Society Hall. The Society Hall belonged to Mr. Hampton Lee. He was another man that you could get to identify you. He was the undertaker-man, and he had a building right across the street from his funeral home. And they met over there for a while. And then some of the churches started opening up and letting them—the Zion United Methodist Church—when the crowd got too big for the Society Hall then we start meeting at Zion. They had a preacher there, Reverend Hogue. And Rev. Hogue was just as interested in the Movement as my husband was. So they started meeting—that's where Dr. King and all of 'em would come and meet over there—at Zion United Methodist Church, and that's where they had Jimmy Lee Jackson's funeral too. And Dr. King preached the funeral eight days after he was shot—he lived and died eight days . . . 'cause the man shot him in his abdomen. At close range.

Did you usually attend the meetings?

Well, at first I did not go because I had young children and I didn't have anybody to leave them with, so I had to stay at home with the children. But Albert never did want me to participate because, he said, if anything happened to him, who gon' be here with the children? Somebody had to be with the children. So I never did get to go to too many, until Albert was two or three years old, and then I used to come up to the mass meetings at Zion with them. But I think I went out to the Sportsman's Club maybe once or twice, but I had to take the kids with me. That was 'bout the only time because like I said, he was afraid something might happen and then both of us would be gone instead of one. So I always was the one to stay in 'cause I never did get arrested.

What was it like for you realizing all the dangers, knowing that you had children and did that ever deter you at all? Or make you want to—

No, 'cause like I said at the time that they was camping out in Selma—they had a lot of people camping out in Selma that was working with the Movement. They just came in to help—students—Albert was the field director for the state of Alabama, so he stayed down there a lot of nights with the students. They slept in Brown Chapel Church and that's where they would sleep. They were coming to help people register to vote. They camped out in the church, they let 'em sleep in the church 'cause there wasn't enough houses where people were afraid to let 'em stay. They were strangers, they didn't know them, so they told 'em that they could stay in the church—and a lot of 'em had their sleeping bags with them, so they just had to go and just find something to eat.

And, so you were well aware of all the dangers and all the—

Yes, sometimes he would tell me about it, and a lot of times he didn't because he didn't want me to worry. And I would call in. Now let's see, Albert was a little baby. He was born in '64. So, that's when everything really broke loose. And he was 'bout five or six months old when Jimmy Lee got shot. 'Cause I had to drive some people down to the hospital.

Yes, the night that Jimmy got shot, my grandmother had the children at the church. We had a big mass meeting, James Orange had been put in jail, and we were going over to the jail to pray with him, and white folks said that we were going out there to break him out of jail. So they had all the state troopers, all the white folks in town deputized as state troopers. Yes—troopers brought in clothes for all of 'em. They just got rid of those things! The guns and everything was where the new James Hood correctional center is now—on the other side of the old jail.

Anyway, that building—they just tore down that old building which housed all the guns and the uniforms that those guys wore that night.

They deputized every white man that would come up there that night. And they lined up from the city hall down to the jail with billy clubs—all the billy clubs in there—and they were beatin' folks that wasn't in the Movement. That didn't have anything to do with it—they got beat that night. If you were black, you got beat. 'Cause some of the people were getting off from M.I. College—the workers. They hadn't even been to a mass meeting—they hadn't been to nothing—and they got beat. Split one man head's open—he was taking some of the workers home on 14. They jumped on him and beat them, and the man said, "Well, why are you beatin' me? I didn't have nothing to do with it!" He said, "You're a nigger, ain't you?" And they beat that man.

They looked over and said, "Oh that's you, Albert!" They did not hit him! Albert had never got beat by no police. Mmm-mmm . . . no.

Wow—they just respected him. So why did they call in all these uniformed—

—'cause they said we was gonna go have a mass meeting that night and break James out of jail—but that was not true. We were going up there to pray with James. And Reverend Dobyne, and O. C. Dobyne and his brother, was leading the line. And when they got to the postoffice, they kneeled down to pray, and, 'cause then they start to walking—the white people start to walking, so they just kneeled down to pray. All the people hadn't got out of the church, 'cause they were still in the church—they were lined up, four deep, and Albert told 'em to line up four deep, and they were going out the door, and they got there by the steps of the post office, then they come just a-beatin' . . . split Mr. Dobyne's head—he never did get over it. . .

His brother, Reverend O.C. didn't get hit that much 'cause he say he knew how to protect himself . . . but his brother was down there praying, and they just beat that poor man. And the news cameras, they busted their cameras—they shot out the lights on the street so couldn't nobody see nothin'. And when they start to beatin' 'em, everyone started to scatterin', you know, . . . some of 'em ran down to the café right in back of the church—that's how they told Jimmy his mom was being beat—so he ran down to the café where his mom was and his ninety-three—eighty-three at that time—year-old grandfather. And when he went to protect his mom, to get her outta there, 'cause she was bleeding from the head 'cause they had hit her in the head. And then one of the old citizens pushed Jimmy up in a corner and that's where he shot him—and he was the grocery store owner—the one that they have in jail now, and they talkin' 'bout Jimmy pulled a knife on him. Jimmy didn't even carry a knife! He didn't have anything in his hand. He was a quiet person. He didn't bother nobody. He didn't say nothin' to nobody. Just because he was trying to get his granddaddy and his momma out of that place, 'cause that's where they ran to . . . they thought they were going to safety . . . and they bust up in that café—just ramshacked it.

Just citizens, not even a trooper.

Mmm-mmm—No! He wasn't no trooper!

I think it's reported that it was a trooper.

He had on trooper clothes, but he wasn't no trooper. All of 'em was dressed up in trooper uniforms, but they weren't troopers. They say he was a trooper, but I was there. I know. And it was the old white man who used to own Piggly Wiggly—the old grocery store down there where Tubbs have his package store at now. That's where Piggly Wiggly was. And old guy used to tell 'em everything that was going on at the meeting. He would come to the meetin' and tell —go back and tell the white folks that was going on. That night he got beat!

They called him "Stit lucky"—he dead now. Didn't have much sense after then . . . they beat him that night. [soft chuckle] He say, "What y'all beatin' me for? I tell y'all what's going on!" They say, "Yeah? You black, ain't you?" They didn't care nothing about him telling what's going on.

Well, why was he doing that?

Crazy! He thought he was doing something telling the white folks what the black folks was doing. He thought he was gaining the white folks' friendship. He thought he was . . . but that night it didn't matter whether he was a friend or not. He got his butt beat. He jumped over . . . in a big old gutter down there by the store . . . he jumped over in there. Another man called "doc Sawyer" . . . [Mocking] "Doc! Doc! Doc!" [laughing] He called everybody "doc" but, he was in it, he was telling everything too. But anyway, they got all of them. And folks that didn't even have nothin' to do with it, they got them too. They just beat everybody.

And how did the night end? Do you remember how things—

Yep, but just before Jimmy got shot, they were trying to come back into the church . . . and I noticed my brother-in-law was there, Lee Curtis, and, um, Willie Lester Martin. Have you talked to Willie Lester? He was a participant—a foot-soldier. A foot-soldier. He stopped them from coming in the building! They put the chairs up behind the doors . . . propped the door up with chairs . . . and they broke a few sitting chairs . . . told 'em if they come in there they wasn't gonna leave out like they came in, so they didn't try to come in. Mmm-hmmm.

And then Jimmy got shot, and then they kept saying "Disperse! Disperse! Go home! Go home!" And somebody yelled, "Well, how in the hell we can go home when y'all standin' out there? Waiting to beat us up!" So Albert told 'em, say, "You all get out the way, then we'll let the folk go home." And then they heard the shot, and then folk was running out the café down there and said, "Jimmy been shot! Jimmy been shot!" and so some guys got him and took him to the hospital in Selma—to Good Samaritan Hospital—that was a Catholic hospital. And they got—they were looking for the guest speaker that night. I think it was Bevel? James Bevel was the speaker. And that's who they were looking for. And they put him in a casket and carried him out to the hearse, and put him in there, so they thought it was a body, and got him out of town.

'Cause they would've shot him.

They would've shot him! And then somebody got Jimmy, 'cause Jimmy stumbled out of the café, up there by the corner of the church. He laid out by the corner of the church.

Mmm-hmmm . . . And they got him and put him in the car and they got him and drove him to Selma. And then I got a carful of people that had gotten beaten or hit or something—they were bleeding. We had a '57 Pontiac. And we had it full. And my grandmother had the three older children and I had the baby. And I carried him on to Selma with me. And I went by Burwell—that's where he was born at—Burwell Hospital—and I took him by there and left him there at the hospital and we carried the rest of the people to Good Samaritan Hospital where they could get treated. And when we could get everybody, Albert saw to everybody getting out and going home, and then we went down to Selma with those folks. Pregnant women lost their babies.

So how would you describe the mood in Marion?

They were mad. They were mad. They boycotted the whole town. They boycotted the whole town. Almost a year! And stores went out of business.

They had to go wherever they could to shop 'cause we didn't allow anybody in the stores—one lady and her family, she had—let me see—about five or six children, and seeing her children walk those streets say, "If you go in that store your hair gonna fall out. I swear upon God your hair gonna fall out." She scared everybody out of the stores.

Yes—people boycotted the stores, you couldn't go in nowhere. And then my husband opened up a store over on Centreville Street where, you know, people that couldn't go anyplace, they could come up there and get groceries. He would haul groceries from Birmingham. We had a fifteen-foot trailer, and he would haul groceries on that cow trail, and he would haul groceries on that to stock the store. We stocked the store. And they would come, and then we would have—we had a guy that would go and buy a fresh beef and have it killed and dressed out, and so we had fresh meat all the time—fresh beef—and they would have a hog killed and then we have fresh pork and stuff like that.

And, well, he set up there, and myself and Miss Ethel Ford, we ran the store for 'em. Her brother was the deputy sheriff. But anyway, we ran the store until we got the Webb place. Mr. Webb let us build his café down there on the other side where the beer garden was. We used that.

Is this the same café where Jimmy Lee was shot?

No—this was on the other end of town—they call it Jefferson Street, down there where Piggly-Wiggly was. We moved down there, and it was a larger place, so we had the pool room and the beer garden—so we operated those too, and we sold over a hundred thousand dollars' worth of grocery.

It was a beer garden there. That's where they sold beer. And then folk come in and play pool and then they go round there and get beer. So we stayed there for a long time, until they felt like they could go back in the white store. Oh that was almost a year—a year and a half—but I know they had gone out of business. Oh yes, the other stores went out of business [too].

Do you know what the racial makeup of the town was at that time?

It was still more blacks than whites—this county has always been more blacks than whites. The only reason they had a lot of whites because of M.I. College and Judson. They started to let them vote. . . . They could vote here or home—so they got them to try to vote here to make their numbers large but it still wasn't larger than the blacks. I used to know the ratios but not anymore.

They would try to go and get the numbers up to where ours was. They would let the college students vote. Mmm-hmm—

they could vote here or either vote at home where they were from, but both colleges insisted on the children voted in this city where they were going to school.

So obviously this was to prevent some kind of majority—

Try to prevent it—but they couldn't because there was more people in the county than it is in the city. Now, we don't have too much luck in the city with the children voting. But if the children don't vote, we beat 'em out every time. 'Cause like this last time in the mayor's race, they won because the students was in session. School was in session so they could vote here.

So during that year of boycotting, a lot happened.

Well a lot of people got registered to vote. We had a federal guy to come in—he was in the bottom of the post office—and he registered a lot of people. I don't remember if he was a black guy. He was—I don't know. 'Cause back then they didn't have too many guys in the federal government who would do that—voter registration. But anyway, they had white people to come in.

Did you participate in the Selma-to-Montgomery marches?

No, I'd just go down and visit on the weekend because I had children and they were going to school so I had to stay at home with the children. But on Fridays I had somebody to pick the children up and I would go down and join them on the march. 'Cause in one of *Ebony*'s magazine I'm on the front page with James Orange as we kneel at the line between Lowndes County and Montgomery County.

It's '65 or '68 . . . but I have on a pink sweater with plaid pants. And I had a collar, you know they used to make these collars—detachable collars—and I had on a white, detachable collar.

And my book got burned up in the house fire. You know I have been trying to get that book but I have not been able to get it 'cause mines got burned up. And I had said that I was going over to my sister's tomorrow because she was a pack-rat. She should have that magazine. 'Cause she was a pack-rat. I wrote and tried to get it from the company, but they never did respond.

So thinking chronologically again, the mood you said—people were angry.

They were angry, and they—'cause before, after Jimmy was shot, the schoolchildren demonstrated. That's when James Orange went out to the school and they demonstrated, and the children got locked up. They took 'em to Selma, they took them to Linden, and they took 'em to Greensboro . . . everywhere a jail was they took the kids there and the parents got upset then . . . and they went to get their kids out and they couldn't get 'em out and they camped out in front of the prison, 'cause they had camped Selma at that time—and my auntie got arrested and she said they had all the ladies in a cell—just put 'em all together in a cell, in a big ol' room, and it had one toilet and they brought a zinc tub in there . . . a big ol' tub for them to get water out . . . that's how they had to drink water.

And so she said all of 'em got put in jail, and that's what they had—and they brought 'em some more half-done peas and cornbread . . . and one lady she was—worked in the cafeteria at school, and she had her pocketbook, and it was loaded with a lot of food! [Laughter]

So they were in jail, and she say, "Come on, Mr. Turner," 'cause he was in Camp Selma, too. She said, "Come on, Mr. Turner, get you something to eat," and she fed him that night. I said, "Lawd have mercy, you ate it?" He said, "Yeah—you ate whatever you could find 'cause you was hungry!"

And so he was one of those who was demonstrating, and he was arrested as well?

Yep . . . when they went to get the children out, they wouldn't let 'em out and folks started to raisin' sand so they just locked him up.

How many times do you think he got arrested during this whole period?

It was quite a few. I can't remember, 'cause he got locked up once in town and I went to get him out. And Damien wouldn't let me get him out. I went in there—the ol' high sheriff, old Bill Loston, and his deputy. His deputy told me to come on in, I was next. And when Bill Loston asked me why was I in there, I said, "Mr. Moody told me to come in," and he stood up there with his ugly self: "No—no he didn't." He didn't tell me to come in there. I said, "Man, you did tell me to come in here!" "Go get at the end of the line!" And it was a line of folks. Just lines. The line was outside of the courthouse. They were coming up there to get their children and their husbands and everybody out of jail. Ooooh! It was a mess. It was one more mess.

When did things quiet down?

Well, the boycott went on and on and on 'til all the stores was just about closed down—Nathan Harris was just about the only one open. And the only reason they were open 'cause M.I. used to buy uniforms from them. So that was the only clothing store. Dimestore had closed, the drugstore had almost closed but you know a lot of folks had to get medicine out of there. But one did close—the RedSaw drugstore—they closed. They closed down, and wasn't nothin' else open but the liquor store, and that was the only one. Wasn't but three stores in town open.

How did all of those—the event of Jimmy Lee Jackson's death, the anger in the town—what did that result in, in terms of mobilizing people to act?

Well, they went to the polls and they voted. We got the black sheriff, we took over the courthouse.

How quickly after all these events was a black sheriff elected?

Let me see. I think he was elected—I think Sheriff Hood was elected in '78 or '79 . . . 'cause he been sheriff for thirty-five years, I believe . . . thirty-five or thirty-six years . . . he's still sheriff. He was just elected sheriff . . . wouldn't nobody run against him, cause little Albert told him ain't no need of you running against Sheriff Hood cause you ain't gonna make it. He told 'em that he say ain't no need. Nobody running against Sheriff Hood, and George Wiggins, and Bobby Singleton.

They were also elected around that time?

Now Bobby Singleton been in there about six or seven years, Bobby Singleton was a little boy then. But he 'bout the youngest one. And Judge Wiggins been in there about four years . . . or longer—things are just now happening, some of them I don't remember because of the stroke. But things that way back I can remember, you know, pretty good—but present events—they kinda foggy. I wouldn't rely on them.

Don't nobody want Judge Wiggins district, 'cause, his counties are too large. 'Cause I know when they call, they had a whole lot of mess over in Greensboro, you know, about his sister being let loose on the voter fraud things, and they had to investigate him and while they was investigating him, a white judge was appointed to run his district—and shoot, that man hurry up and told 'em to let Judge Wiggins come back because he could not handle it! Shoot, he couldn't handle it. So wouldn't nobody run against him 'cause they wouldn't want to have to work his district.

Why were they—

It's too large. I forgot exactly how many counties. I know he's in Dallas . . . he's in Wilcox counties—the whole Black Belt—he works that.

Well, we got satisfied when we got a black sheriff. Got a black sheriff, took over the courthouse—every office in the courthouse. Then the Board of Education. All of them are black now that whites have someone to represent them from their neighborhood like up in Heiberger, they got a white person. I don't think they have but one white person on the board. The rest is black. And the health department, they have some white doctors come in, students, nurses, and stuff. I mean, pharmacists, they from Samford University. They were here Saturday, 'cause they had the health fair uptown. We the only county [to] observe Obama's day.

So when I hear you say that you finally got a black sheriff in the late seventies, I'm thinking, well that's a long time to wait! Did it seem that way to you?

Well, we had gotten some blacks elected, but the sheriff was a big thing. We had gotten some blacks elected, but the sheriff was putting icing on the cake.

That was seen as evidence of progress.

Mmm-hmmm—of voting, of all we had gone through. That was a significant thing. We had black superintendents. Mr. Ernest Palmer—he was the first. He lives in Tuscaloosa. And back when the whites was in control of the Board of Education, all the teachers had to go to Wilburn Brothers—that was one of the stores here in Marion. They had to go buy furniture and clothes from them, and they had to get their groceries from the store. I bought the store and done forgot the name—we bought the building. I purchased the building.

But everybody had to go over there and buy your groceries. That's where you had to take up your groceries, and you pay 'em every month when you get paid off. And the teachers, they would make the teachers wait 'til 12 o'clock on Saturdays to get their checks. It was a white store.

It was a white store. . . . Oh and they made the teachers wait . . .

Mmm-hmmm—'til Saturday, and then the superintendent would give the checks to the—to the head supervisor—black lady. They said she was goin' with the man, but I don't know about that. But anyway, she used to get the checks, but she couldn't give 'em out 'til 12:00, that's after the bank had closed. Marshall Polk—that was the name of the grocery store. You had to get your grocery from Marshall Polk. Everybody. All the teachers.

What happened to your grocery store at that time?

Oh we hadn't started it then. That was before—that was back in the fifties. Oh, I'm going back! [Chuckles] Oh, this is back in the fifties, and all the teachers had to get their groceries from Marshall Polk grocery, and then you get your clothes from Wilburn Brothers, and your furniture from Wilburn Brothers. They had a big store. They got it named now—Sowing Seeds of Hope? Oh, what the name of that place now? It's downtown, but that's the building they house now, that was Wilburn Brothers. And so he had built a Marion Motel? He had stock in that, and he said when a black person go in there, he was gon' kill hisself.

So my sister-in-law and my brother-in-law got married. And I was working then as a social worker for Berean Headstart, and my sister-in-law and I paid for my brother-in-law's room at the Marion Motel. [laughter] We was gon' see if he was gon' cut his throat. Sure enough he did! They went in the bathroom that morning—he was in there. Had drowned in his own blood—sure had—at his home. He had started going down from there, then they finally closed. Sure did. I said, "I'm gon' make him out a liar!" [laughter] Mmm-hmmm! He said wasn't no niggas gonna stay in that hotel! But they sure spent their honeymoon that night in the Marion Motel. It was brand new then.

Just like the Webb brothers. After they set my house afire and we got acquitted in court, they couldn't send us off that way. So they set the house afire. They said we can't run 'em out of town so we'll burn 'em out. So they set the house afire and Albert still got off, and they couldn't run us off. Albert told 'em he was gonna be buried in Marion, so they just might as well stop all their plotting because he wasn't going nowhere, and he didn't go nowhere 'til 2000 and that's when he died—and he buried out there on Highway 14, on their grandpa's land.

Can you say a little about what the social relationships were like between blacks and whites during that period of time when you were waiting to elect black officials into public office?

Some of them killed themselves, some of them moved down to Gulf Shores—lot of them moved down there cause they had an old lawyer—every time I go over there to see my brother, his big, two-story house is facing his house. Berks—that's his name—Lawyer Berks and he moved to Gulf Shores. And the city manager of Marion—he moved. He made Billingsley slip by his house. He's another Uncle Tom.

I'm really interested in hearing about the [Turner] trial.

It's in the July issue of *Jet*'s magazine and the *Ebony* magazine. . . 'cause the trial went on for four weeks. So *Jets* wrote about it every week.

And the trial wasn't nothing—they had amateurs. Old Jeff Session—he was the prosecutor, and I had Chestnut Sanders and Sanders, my lawyers.

Yeah, they were my lawyers, and then after two weeks into the trial, the constitution lawyers came down from New York and they represented me. My husband and I had to get separate lawyers—they would not let us have the same lawyers.

Why were you both being tried separately?

They said that we had messed with the election—we was setting up the election. We had got folks to vote the way we wanted them to vote.

And this was a national election? What election were they talking about?

Uh, they were talking about the sheriff election and the national election.

The presidential or senators?

The senators.

Like a midterm election?

Mmm-hmm.

'Cause it happened, no, that was the national cause it was in November and the trial didn't come up until that summer—June—they had started in January prosecuting people, getting people all riled up, 'cause we had to go to Mobile 'cause my husband was in the hospital at the time—'cause they had accused him and Mr. Earl Ford, but Mr. Earl Ford was working. He was—he owed some big white man some money so they took him off and they had a certain number of people so they just stuck me on there.

You mean a certain number of people they were charging for this?

Mmm-hmm, 'cause they had three of us . . . it was supposed to be Earl Ford, Albert Turner, and Spencer Hogue. Okay, because Spencer—I mean, Earl owed this man a whole lot of money, they took him off. So they said, well, let's put Albert's wife on. And so they put me on.

And then this white lady said I brought a man there, in her office, to vote absentee. And the man was getting ready to go out of town, so I told him, I said, well, come on. I was working upstairs for the district judge, and I told him I said, well, come on I'll take you downstairs and you can vote now if you're gonna be out of town. And I went down there and she claim I took off on the judge's time. I said, "Well, the judge wasn't there!" And the judge didn't have no court case comin' up, so I was just there sitting in the office answering the telephone!

Was this a white woman?

Mmm-hmmm . . . old bent-over one. She kept a lot of mess-ups going, 'cause she told me I didn't have no business coming down there 'cause I was on state time. And I said well the state wasn't doing nothing! So I came down and got this man to register to vote, and get rid of you! And that's when we got the probate judge and the county clerk.

A black clerk?

We got the first black circuit clerk.

Was it the same time that the judge was brought in also?

Mmm-hmmm . . . yeah.

So '78, '79 was big . . .

Oh yes, honey.

When were you charged?

We was charged in, well, we had the election in November—the past November, and so they didn't take office until January. And then they start—they charged us in December—after the election. They charged Earl and them. I didn't get charged until later, the next year, but they started in '84, call themselves getting witnesses—getting up witnesses, and stuff like that. And we—when we first went to trial, we went to trial in March, I believe. We started off in Mobile, 'cause they carried—they had two busloads of us going to Mobile. Called themselves they had witnesses and people that would have voted absentee and stuff like that—and we went to Mobile, and we had the town drunk on the bus, and the DA come telling me, "Evelyn, now, you don't let Marvin have no drink." I said, "Look, lady, I'm not taking care of nobody but Evelyn Turner. You know what Marvin was 'fore you got him so you take care of him—I'm not taking care of him," and I didn't! And [giggles] one of the guys went and bought a fifth of liquor. [laughter] He gave it to Marvin, and he wasn't even able to testify! He didn't know what he was testifying to no way! So they was wanting him to say that he was paid to do it—Albert had paid him to vote—but his mom was a big civil rights worker, so he knew what he was supposed to do, so he did.

But anyway, we went to Mobile, and they talking about we stayed there two or three days—then they said we were gon' have to pay for our food and all that, and we told the judge, "We didn't have no money to pay for no food! Y'all brought us down here on some humbug—and, we didn't ask to come down here!" So they let us go back. We left that night—bus brought us back to town, and then they said they were gonna try to sober up Marvin, but they never did sober him up. [laughter] So he couldn't even testify. So they were talking 'bout we had to go to the court—federal building down there in Selma—and that's where they moved the trial, down there in Selma. And every day, folks from everywhere would come to hear the trial and Ty, Chess, and them. And Chess was a ball of fire.

Jail Chestnut. He's got the largest law firm in Selma. Black law firm. But that's who represented my husband. And Chestnut was Albert's lawyers, and Hank Sanders was my lawyer, but they were from the same firm so they said we had to get different lawyers. So they had the people up north was hearing about the trial and they sent the constitutional lawyers down to defend me and Spencer. So that was alright for them to do. So, they were in court—we were in court—up until the 4th of July. Every day went to the court. I think my house was burned the last week of the trial—'cause the trial lasted four weeks.

And the last week my house got burned, and the lawyer closed the court for two days because everybody came to court smelled like fire—you know, smoke. And he said we couldn't do that because we'd sway the jury. So somebody would bring—my auntie was the seamstress—and they would bring material to her house to make my clothes so I would have a new dress—and one lady came and opened up her trunk. She had a trunk of shoes, and she told me to pick out any pair I wanted—I said, well, black go with everything so I got a pair of black shoes—and some guy brought Albert some suits for him to wear—'cause when he got out of the hospital he had lost a lotta weight, so he could get in them.

And we came on back to court . . . and it was one guy there—I don't know who that man was but he was a juror, and he would be looking at me winking his eye, and I would wink back at him. [Laughter]

The DA was such a funny bunch of folks, so, the judge called the justice department and said y'all need to call somebody to come down here and conduct this trial 'cause this is nothing but a kangaroo court.

This was a black judge.

No, he was white. He just knew they had no evidence! 'Cause they had ballots that had been erased with just ink—just scratched out—and they had done that! And they was trying to put it on us! They were just low-down—yeah—'cause we were just getting rid of so many people—'cause the DA office was the only office in the courthouse that wasn't black.

So, 'cause everybody was saying, "Well, we need to have some whites up there. . . ." The DA office's all we need, so that's the only office up there that wasn't black. And so—

So, that's a huge accomplishment to have gotten all those offices filled by black people.

Mm-hmmm—tax collector, tax assessor. They was mad!

So we had one old black guy that we had elected to office. He worked in the office where we pay taxes. Tax assessor—that's what he was. And he got on the witness stand and lied and said that Albert Jr. had come to him for a job . . . and Albert Jr. was just eight years old. And honey when he said that, Chestnut just tore him up! Tore him up.

When he cross-examined him?

Mmm-hmmm! Yes. Say he had come to him for a job. So Chess told him, he should turn him up to the labor cause they hiring eight-year-old boys to work in his office! "Naw, Naw, he wasn't the one!" He said, "Well, you done lied twice, then, 'cause you said Albert Jr. came there, and Albert Jr.'s just eight years old!" So he just tore him up. So that's the reason the judge say it was just a circus going on there.

So at one point in the trial was your house burned?

Almost—the last week . . . Mmm-hmmm. They said, well, we couldn't put him out of. Couldn't send to prison—Burn him out. 'Cause his cook came down and told us . . . she couldn't get in touch with us—she had been trying to get in touch with us but we were in Selma all day at the courthouse, so she went and told the sheriff, so the sheriff got in touch with us.

But that day I had to go by the doctor's office, 'cause Albert thought I was losing my mind.

Anyway, they couldn't get in touch with us, so that night we got home and the lawyer came over the house . . . our lawyer, my lawyer and our friend, the deputy sheriff 'cause they had to come over, too. And they were in the kitchen—talking, going over strategy—what they were gonna do and everything, and the doctor had given me a sedative so I had gone to bed. I was in the bedroom and they were in the kitchen talking, and Earl Ford said, "Albert, I smell smoke!" And this lady 'cross the road from me—she was an old lady—she said, "There's two white mens out there in your backyard with a can."

She called and told—I answered the phone. And I said, okay—thank you—just like that. And after a while we smelled smoke, and then Earl said, "I smell smoke!" and Albert said, "Oh that's somebody burning something—burning leaves or something." And so after a while, it got stronger and stronger. They threw a [inaudible] cocktail on the roof of the house, and we had shingles. And it exploded—they had already threw one up under the car so they could say the car set the house on fire. But the fire marshal said it started from the roof in the kitchen 'cause a big hole was burning up there in the kitchen. And so Earl opened the back door. When he opened up the back door, the car exploded, and he slammed the door, and Albert and them ran out the front door. Then he thought about me being in the back room and said, "Earl, go back there and get my wife—my wife in the bed!" So Earl came back there in the back—he say, "Get up, Evelyn, Get up! Get up! The house on fire!" I went to get my robe, and he say, "You ain't got time to get no shoes, just come on!" I ran down the driveway and he ran down the driveway, and in my bathrobe, I ran across the street to the old lady's over cross the street. And I was crying and I didn't have on any shoes. She gave me some kind of shoes to put on my feet and when the fire truck got there, they just sprayed water all over the house—even where the fire was—they just messed up all my clothes and furniture and stuff. And so the old fire chief [said], "Dag . . . they tried to burn you out, didn't they!" with his old dumb self. He dead and in hell now. For real.

But that's what he hollered. And I bust out and started crying and then I told Albert I wanted to leave. . . . I didn't want to stay here no more. And he told me I couldn't be talking like this. My brother-in-law live right up the street, so we went up there and we spent the night up there.

And then the next day we went to court. The lady across the street would fix breakfast for us every morning, but you just couldn't eat breakfast.

And folks getting up there on the witness stand deliberately lying—and one lady talking 'bout, she didn't care nothing 'bout me—she wish they would throw me in jail and throw the keys away. This a black woman saying this!

These were black people! That was a black woman . . . said they would put me in jail and throw the key away! She just didn't like me. And I never did anything to her 'cause she was part of Albert's family and I used to go visit her, you know. So I asked the man that stay next door to her, I said, "Well, why would she say things like that?" He said, "Evelyn, you don't know how many women are jealous of you."

I said, "Jealous of me for what? I don't have anything!" He said, "Huh, the way you wear your clothes and the way you walk, you just walk like you own the whole world!" I said, "Well, I just walk like that . . . and I . . . just don't pay that any attention and just go ahead on!" Oh child, he said, "They just don't like you."

I'm sure the prosecutors knew it looks bad to have black people speaking against you.

Had a whole lot of them. A lot of them. And then we had a lot of people, 'cause see we used to help a lot of people. Because we had the store, and then when they got the food stamps and them, Albert and them marched. When the poor people train went to Washington, DC, they went up there for the poor people and then we got the food stamps. And so when we got back home, when he got back home, a lot of people didn't know anything about food stamps. He took his car and drove around in different communities. He had different people in those communities to go get people and bring them up to the food stamps office and get food stamps. If they didn't have any money, like some of them had to pay five dollars—fifteen dollars—if they didn't have it, he would give it to them so they could purchase the food stamps and then they could get food for their families. See, and then they thought these people were gonna go against us. And one lady told them say, "No—ain't nobody gon' make me go against Albert Turner. He fed me when I didn't have nothing. My children didn't have nothing. He brought turkeys over there to the house. He gave during the Christmas and Thanksgiving 'cause we didn't have anything to eat. Naw, I ain't going against Mr. Turner. Whatever he wanted me to do, I did it, and I did it on my own. . . ." And so different ones said that, you know.

This man had twelve or sixteen children. He [Albert] drove over there and got him and brought him to the food stamps office, and he got five hundred dollars worth of food stamps. And he could feed his family. And we had the store—if they wanted to come, they would come to the store, say, "We goin' to your store, Mr. Turner." But it wasn't his store, it was the community store. And they would buy food, and they would get all the groceries they could carry.

Yeah . . . and when they needed money they could come and always get money from him. He didn't charge us no interest on no money. Whatever we needed—if he had it, he could get it. They could get it. And Spencer Hogue was the same way.

And remind me again who Spencer Hogue is?

He had a stroke. He was one of the Marion three that was in the trial.

Was he also part of the Movement?

Oh he was a part of the Movement. He was a real big, 'cause he was the treasurer for the Movement, you know. Yeah . . . Spencer was deep off in it and his children, too, was one of the first ones went over to integrate the school.

And so the trial ended after how many months?

We ended on July the 4th. We was acquitted—all three of us was acquitted. It's in the *Jet* magazine. I had on a red dress. It's down there in the Selma museum now. Mmm-hmmm. A red dress. My auntie had made it. And the top was polka-dot black and white, and I had a red jacket that matched the skirt and I had on that lady's black shoes! [Laughter] We on the front in the *Jet*. I don't know, now I don't think we were on the front, but I know we were in the *Jet*. I was laughing, and Chestnut was holding up my hand I believe, and Malika, Hank's daughter, was standing right beside me.

Wow—that's a big day.

Ooooh, it was, honey! We could go home and eat some watermelon and ribs. We had to go to court on July the 4th.

How long did it take before the jury gave a decision?

I don't know . . . was it two hours? How long—I know they came out cause the jury wanted to go home and eat some watermelon and barbeque too! 'Cause they had to stay there. But they got through and they said everything was "not guilty." All the criminal charges—we had a hundred something.

And the judge didn't want the folks to holler out, but he couldn't do nothing.

How'd the town react?

Oh honey, they just hollered. Oh, and they sung freedom songs. They did, "Ain't gon' nobody turn us around," and they just sung everything. That was a glorious day. 'Cause we had been going to trial—least, I had been going to trial ever since March—'cause he was in the hospital, and so I had to go to trial and they had me down there asking me all kinda old stupid questions . . . "was I going with the judge" and "the judge bought me a pair of topaz earrings." I told 'em my ear wouldn't know how to act with a pair of topaz diamond earrings! No way—no! I said the judge bought his wife a pair, and I saw him and he told me to try 'em on. He said, "Oh Ms. Turner that looks so beautiful against your skin. . . ." [giggling] I said but they weren't mine, sir. Yeah, "and you're always taking up for the judge." I said, "That was my job, to take up for the judge," 'cause the judge was sickly and cause he used to have epilepsies.

This was the judge you worked for?

Mmm-hmmm. I was his secretary for eight years, and he would—they would say he was drunk, but he would be having seizures, 'cause that old woman down there was saying that he would be drunk. That old, old circuit clerk woman. They used to pick at him all the time. But I always get him out of it.

Well, that is quite a culmination. I'm sure the town as a whole reacted. How about white reaction generally?

They wasn't doing nothing. 'Cause they was afraid! They didn't know how the blacks . . . they thought the blacks would treat them like they had treated us. But we didn't. I told 'em. . . . Y'all won't, but I will. . . .

Were you ever trained in nonviolent methods?

Mmm-mmm.

Did that training come here [to Marion]?

Yeah, they had training, 'cause a guy called Pat Davis—was one of the ones that was training in nonviolence. And they was showing them how they should duck when the folk be trying to hit you in the head. How you supposed to protect yourself. I was never out there 'cause Turner did not let me take a part in that.

So your husband was trained in those methods . . . ?

Yep—and he knew how to protect hisself.

They had a group from Atlanta would come down and train them—the nonviolence group that would come down and train and they had training in all of the counties—the Black Belt. . . .

And so your husband—how was he connected to Martin Luther King? Did they work closely together?

Very closely—'cause he had the whole Black-Belt county—the state of Alabama. And he had, I think, fifty or sixty people working under him. And he would just tell them whatever Martin wanted him to do, he would relay it to the workers, and they would carry it out. 'Cause they had whites working with him too. 'Cause you know we used to have to take a test before we could vote.

Asking you how many stars in the flag, how many stripes in the flag—and what was the capital, Washington, DC—just all kind of old stupid questions. And the folks that was giving the test didn't even know 'em.

'Cause I know they had the old judge up there—the old probate judge and he just finished the third grade so you know darn well he didn't know how to answer nothing.

And they said, why would you have a judge with just a third-grade education, and you got two colleges here in Marion—M.I. College and Judson College, and got a third-grade judge sitting up there? So they got shamed. So that [other] judge, he wasn't no better. But he did finish high school. They got him out—the last time we had an election, before this time, we elected a black lady probate judge.

Oh wow—she the first?

She's the first. Mmm-hmmm. Ms. Eldora Anderson. So she went back to school. Her son is the chief of police in Tuscaloosa. Now I knew her parents—her mom just died last year—but they instilled in those children to go to church. They were real Christian people. She brought her children up just like her parents brought her up.

I've been curious about the role that Christian faith played in the civil rights movement and then for you, specifically.

Ever since you had our revival, and then you had to get on the mourner's bench. And the old people believed in that and you could get someone—get a member of the church to pray with you while you on the mourner's bench. And, religion is real high—it was high in school, 'cause in the morning time when we got to school, we had devotion and a prayer. Yep—in the fifties. Mmm-hmmm—we had to have devotion every morning. Each class would have their devotion and they would pray.

Do you think it strengthened your resolve throughout the Movement? Did it give you personally a sense of peace and strength—

Well, I had it before then—before the Movement—'cause my grandmother told us about the Bible. Like I said, my husband taught the Bible at the church and we just always felt like God wasn't gonna bless you if you didn't go hear the word of God. You have to go to church. And they didn't send you to church, they took you to church—and like that song said—if you act like you didn't want to go to church your grandparents—your momma would "drag you to church." [Laughter] My grandmomma didn't have to do nothing but looked at us over her glasses and you know what that mean—get in there to Sunday school. Mmm-hmmm. Yep. Religion played a big part in our lives.

And, do you remember the day that Martin Luther King died? And what was that like?

Oooh—that was the worst day. People in the big cities was setting everything on fire and the folks down South was just praying.

And where were you?

I was at home. And Albert was at home. And they called and told him that Martin had been shot. So he left the next day going to Memphis. And I wanted to go to the funeral, so he sent a car down for me and I went to Atlanta. There was so many people, and by me being so short I couldn't see anything. So we went up to the hotel where we were going to spend the night 'cause Albert is leading the mule in the funeral procession. He the big man. And I went up to the hotel and that's where I could see everything because we had television. We saw it on television.

What was the mood and the atmosphere?

Just everybody was sad. Everybody was crying. And those that weren't crying, they was angry, they was tearing up everything. It was just—it was just disastrous. It really was.

Were you shocked?

Yes.

Did you have a sense it would happen?

No, I never thought nothing like that would happen. But it did. I didn't do anything that day, just sat there glued at the television, same way it was when President Kennedy got shot. I said, "Oh no, not again."

Wow. What about his brother, when Bobby Kennedy was shot?

Yeah, Bobby got shot.

What were you thinking at that time?

The world was just gone to the dogs. Not the world, but the people in the world, 'cause God made the world. And I said the people in the world has just gone to the dogs. Oooh! That was a terrible, terrible time.

Did you know Coretta Scott King?

Mmm-hmmm. She lived here in Perry County—in North Perry, really.

I'm just amazed at how much history is in this town.

It's a lot. And they tried to get Albert to write a book before he died, but he never would. He didn't like being out, you know. He wanted the whole community to be a part of whatever. He didn't want no praise. He didn't ever wear buttons—nothing flashy. He was just a plain old country boy, and we used to, when we'd get ready to go to church, I used to get after him about putting on different things [chuckles] he didn't want. He talking 'bout matching it up. He didn't think about nothing like that. He just put it on!

And he was sick when he passed away?

Oh yes. Albert had a number of things, he had emphysema, he had asthma, and high blood pressure—they just named a number of things that he had, so they just put on the death certificate of natural causes. But when he was in the Movement, they slept out in the rain and in the mud and the cold—whatever—'cause he said they were so cold in Washington when they went up there on the Poor People's Campaign. Sometimes his feet got wet and he had to keep the socks on and the shoes. So it was just a primitive life.

Johnny Flowers

Johnny Flowers, an African-American business owner and politician from Uniontown, Alabama, discusses his participation in the Selma-to-Montgomery march. He also discusses race relations in Uniontown versus Marion and his perspective on the sometimes-volatile relationship between black politicians and community leaders in Perry County. He covers his own lengthy political career extending into the 1990s. In his testimony, Mr. Flowers tells powerful stories that lend insight into the dynamics between blacks in Marion and Uniontown which, from his perspective, stemmed from the civil rights era and the marches from Selma to Montgomery. He speaks to the political tensions that resulted in Perry County, and how he believes he helped bridge the divide. Among the notable names mentioned in this oral history are Jimmy Lee Jackson, Albert Turner Sr., Viola Liuzzo, Andrew Hayden, and Andrew Young.

☐ ☐ ☐

You will find my story different. It's not a story—my history of Perry County is different from probably anybody you'll talk to, because I'm on both sides of the coin and I'm more liberal to talk to you about some of the negative parts of it. It's amazing.

I know you've heard a lot about the civil rights era of the South. But I am a product of the black part of the history—you might look at the civil rights era as white against black? You'd be surprised how much black against black there was. And you will hear my side of that part of the story—and you'll be amazed.

It's interesting. And I am a product of it. This is not a hearsay story. This is an actual story that took place during that era, 1965 and '66, when I was in high school. And I got involved into the Movement, in Uniontown, Alabama.

Uniontown was—and Marion was—divided. And where the Marion side boycotted and marched and all that sort of stuff, the Uniontown [side]—a lot of the black people had their own businesses, they did not want to march—they didn't see any need for it. And so you had a divide. Even with this county, within the black people.

Why didn't they feel a need?

Well, like I said, they had their own businesses and they was more, uh, I'll use the term "independent blacks" that had their own businesses and they felt that they were more freer, you see. And they looked at themselves as not needing to march or not needing to boycott, or not needing to take the streets.

So they didn't have a sense that there was an injustice happening to them?

Oh, they was part of the injustice, but, their viewpoint of it was more—I'll use the term, relaxed attitude. Oh, they was called "the word" and went through the whole process, but in Uniontown you had some business and cafés and you know, grocery stores owned by blacks, so it was a different spirit, you see, when it came to economics. So they felt that the need for us to be in the streets, marching, and doing whatever, was not necessary. So they felt although they was discriminated against, and they was mistreated like everybody else. But in that little world of theirs, they had their own stores. They had their own grocery stores, so it was more of a freedom, you might say, involved in the Uniontown area than in Marion.

Before you say that, did you grow up in Uniontown?

Born and raised—still there!

During the march, when the Albert Turners and the stuff that happened here with Jimmy Lee Jackson—I and a friend of mine—his name was Charles White—he's in Boston, Massachusetts. He was living next to me in Uniontown, Alabama, and my dad was an old Baptist preacher. Charles was kind of into what was happening. He was probably two years older, and I was only about sixteen. Charles was here the night that Jimmy Lee got killed—he was here from Uniontown. So when they was organizing the march to march from Selma to Montgomery, Charles rode to Selma with my dad. My dad was pastoring a church there. And Charles was all prepared to march and the whole nine yards—and so when I got to Selma, I said, "Well, Dad, can I go?" I was only sixteen, and he says, "Sure, go ahead." We had no idea—had no idea! But Charles was all ready. Had his little sack and his little lunch bucket, and he was ready to march! Where I just went to church dressed up in my necktie and coat. But yet, Dad said, "Sure, go ahead!"

Dad. My dad was probably the only minister in Uniontown, Alabama—black minister—that was kind of into what was happening in the civil rights era. And so Daddy was involved. He was going to the mass meeting. Not all of them, but he was involved. So he said, "Sure!"

So I went in there. But, to make the story kind of interesting . . . you know where we went over the bridge, and there was all the tear gas, and because we was from Perry County, all of the people from Perry County was down front. So we was over the bridge. It wasn't a situation that we were on the other side. We was down front, 'cause we was from Perry County. And so all the tear gas and all that crack in the heads and all that—that's where we were, on the other side. That's where we were. So we suffered the major blow of what happened that day of Bloody Sunday.

So, we went through the thing that night, and the horses and the bridge and all that. Charles and I spent the night with some guy in Selma. I have no idea who he was but I spent the night with him. And my dad, because pastoring in Selma, had a member there. So quite naturally early the next morning after we woke up from this guy's house, I contacted her and my mom and dad. I couldn't image what they went through that night not knowing what had happened to me.

And they knew what kind of person I was—they knew I was down front. I mean, they could imagine, 'cause they knew me! Anyway, I contact Ms. Manual, that was her name . . . and quite naturally she fed me breakfast that morning. Charles contacted my dad by telephone and let 'em know I was alright and everything is well.

Now, I get home, and Dad says, "You're not going back—you're not gonna march anymore! I'm not gonna let you!" Charles White came when he was getting ready to organize the other march—the real one—and he said to my dad, "Rhett—are you going to take me back this Sunday so I can march?" and he says, "No, I'm not gonna do it! I don't want you all to get hurt!" And Charles said to Dad, "If you don't drive me to Selma, I'm going to . . ." Selma is thirty miles from Uniontown. He said, "I'm gonna walk from Uniontown to Selma . . . to walk to Montgomery!" And Dad said, "Well . . . okay. I'll drive you." And quite naturally, I wanted to go. My brother says, "I wanna go!" I have another brother, two years younger than I, Charles White had another brother, two years younger than he, and then we had a first cousin. It was only five of us from Uniontown, along with my dad. The only people during that whole process going from Uniontown—the only ones—where Marion had a huge amount of people. But Uniontown only had five young boys, and one preacher.

Did others—other blacks in Uniontown know what was happening?

Sure! It was just like this Albert Turner thing. Albert Turner was leading in Marion, and Andrew Hayden was leading in Uniontown. And Andrew Hayden was—"We don't need to march. . . ." You know, I mean he had his own [inaudible] with James Brown and all of the people coming down performing. Two different worlds!

And so, he had this business on Saturday night and he was making—it was just two different worlds altogether. And so he was like, "We in Uniontown don't have to go through this process. I mean, we don't have to because . . . we don't have any problems like the folks in Marion."

So Hayden and Albert Turner was a divide, and the county was divided on those two people. You had Uniontown people saying, "Oh—we're already free—we don't have to deal with this." And then the Marion people saying, "What in the world—those crazy people in Uniontown!" So you had . . . so five young boys and a preacher who is known for his hoopalastic hollerin',—I mean, he's not educated.

So Daddy called us, and we went back to Selma, and we were in this march. And, 'course the story along the way is just more than you can imagine.

There was a young lady—I'd love to know where she is now— She walked until her feet got blistered and I guess water was on the bottom of her feet that thick [gestures]—and they was carrying her into one of these trailer houses where the doctors and all treat your feet. And they carried her in and they worked on her feet. And they brought her out, holding her up, and she said, "You put me down. I want to walk!" And they said, "You can't walk, your feet is too sore!" And she says, "I gotta walk!" I would love to meet her now and find out—that's how serious...

I mentioned this the other day because we lost the election— the vote—and all the Democrats lost because black people didn't go to the voting polls . . .

But anyway . . . we went to the march and we marched. Came back, had my little red jacket—all six of us had our red jackets where we marched all the way.

What was the significance of the red jackets?

Oh! Nobody didn't tell you? Okay—

We left Selma, going to Montgomery—lotta people—by the thousands. But when you got to the Lowndes County line the highway instead of being two lanes, became one. So they wouldn't allow but three hundred people to march. Wasn't but three hundred people allowed to march all the way through Lowndes County, 'cause you only had one highway, so you had to put people marching in one lane in the traffic—they let so many go east and so many go west. So, couldn't but three hundred of us march all of the way. Totally. So, when we get to the Lowndes County line and all these thousands of people—so now you got to separate who go all the way, and who go back!

And those who go back so many journalists on the other side so many days later—to continue to march, but can't but three hundred people march through Lowndes County all of the way! So Mr. Turner, five of us from Uniontown, Alabama—we get to the line and Mr. Turner says, "Get out of the line, you guys from Uniontown!"

And—I love this part [chuckling]—Charles White, who was kind of our leader, 'cause if it wasn't for him we wouldn't be there. He says, "We're not gonna get out—we're the only five from Uniontown, Alabama, and we deserve to march all the way!" And Mr. Turner says, "You all in Uniontown say you free! Get out! Get out of this line!" And so it became a big roar. Here this little boy, Charles White—Charles about eighteen—and here's this man, Albert Turner, and it got to be a war, and Charles says, "You all sit down!" So we boycotted—we set down at that Lowndes County line and wouldn't get out of the line. And by this time it was such a roar. Andrew Young came back and says, "What's wrong?" And Charles explained that Albert Turner says, "You from Uniontown, Alabama! They say they already free they need to get out of the line! Can't but three hundred go!" And Charles White says, "But we're the only six from Uniontown, Alabama!" And Albert Turner says, "But people in Uniontown say they're free!" And Charles White says, "But we sits here to let you know that we in Uniontown is not free."

Johnny Flowers

And then the people in line began to yell, "Let 'em go! Let 'em go!" These other folk are going back. Andrew Young said finally, you know, and I guess there was. . . . Albert Turner was like a sergeant and Andrew Young was like a lieutenant. And so Andrew Young says, "Let them go. Let them march." So they gave us opportunity then to let us march all of the way.

So everybody that marched all the way received a little orange jacket. Like a little vest. And we had all the songs written on the vest, you know, that we sung along the way. Now we went over to the march and we marched all the way and we spent the night and were at St. Jude and the stage collapsed with Peter, Paul, and Mary on it and finally Daddy said, "We're gonna go home." This was over and Dad was a preacher—and Daddy's job was hauling people back and forth, by the way. He stayed aboard, hauled black folks, white folks back and forth from Selma. This particular night Daddy said I'm gonna take my children, and I'm not gonna haul anybody else back home. We're gonna take you all back home. This is Dad. So we got in the car and we came on back. Coming through Lowndes County they stopped us. Bust out his tail light on his car, "Nigga, don't you know you don't have any tail light?" and Dad said, "No—I don't have any now!"

We was probably one car—I'm almost sure—ahead of Viola Liuzzo, when she got killed behind us. Because when we got to the church, when we drove up, the word was, they just killed Viola Liuzzo in Lowndes County, so it had to have been we was just in front of her.

Now—that part of the story. We get home, after the march, and we have these little red jackets. And we wanted to wear our red jackets to school the next day. And Dad says, "No, you all can't wear those red jackets—you can't do it." So we couldn't wear our red jackets. Daddy knew and we knew—we couldn't wear 'em uptown because Uniontown and these red jackets says that you walked all the way from Selma to Montgomery. "You all only six—you can't do it!" So we couldn't wear them.

Prior to going to the march I was probably an A-student in Perry County school system. After that march I became a "D" and a "F." And then, I filled out an application to go to A&M University. I typed up another friend of mine's—he came to Dad's house, and I typed up his application and I typed up mines. I put a ten-dollar bill in that application, gave it to the councilman. He ended up going up to A&M University. Mine got thrown in the back of the pile. I had no idea why I wasn't accepted to A&M. I worked that summer to get me some money to go to college, but all of a sudden I never made it. 'Course I went into the military and the whole nine yards, and I met my wife some years later and she went to work at that school and when I met her she wanted to find out more of who I was.

We was dating and she knew the best way to find out more about me was to go into my file in the school. Guess what? She found out that my application and the whole nine yards was thrown in that school—back then, you couldn't go in and dig up your records. Only now you can do it but you couldn't do it then. It was private information. But by she was working there, she went and she came back to me. She says, "Somebody didn't like you," and I say, "What you mean?" Then she told a story about my application, how I filed to go ahead in university and it end up in the school records.

I was tracked. And it all happened because—and if you ask me why, it's because I went on that march. Can you imagine? But it happened in that school system and it happened to me and maybe it did happen over the march and maybe it didn't—I don't know. But it happened. If you ask me it happened because I went on the march. But a lot of kids was tracked during that time and a lot of kids was treated like that. It didn't hurt me—I ended up being very successful and, what can I say? I didn't need the college education. I survived without it. But, whatever happened to me happened to me. Can you imagine? So, what I'm telling you now is, the civil rights era, a lot of people was mistreated by whites, but I'm a product of being [mis]treated by blacks. [Laughs]

Ain't that something? Can you imagine? And even to this day, in Uniontown, Alabama. Black History Month and the whole stuff that goes along with the story of it all. You think I've ever been invited to speak in Uniontown? On black history? Never.

Even now down there, people in Marion—I think I've spoken once up here, maybe, but never in a Black History program in Uniontown, Alabama, have I been invited to talk. Now, there's a whole lot that goes on and with that . . . for eighteen years, I went in the military—I'm a military vet, I have my own construction company, I've never been employed by anybody but me, I mean there's more to my life than just—you understand.

If you ask me, I think I've done well. I live in a small community, but I don't think small. And I don't live small. I think that's part of why I'm maybe not asked to talk. Some of the same people that was there that taught me during that high school period is still there. You know. Still living there—they've seen me go from the guy that didn't go to college to the guy that we've had to make a loan from this very same individual. Can you imagine?

Ain't that something? And they're still there, and they wouldn't dare let me get up and tell my story, because they was part of the history of the story. So why would they want me to tell that I didn't go to A&M story and graduate because my file got put back in the folder at the school that these people here was teaching me during the time. Interesting, isn't it? [Laughs] Isn't that something! But it didn't hurt me. But that's part of the civil rights story that very few people really understand. And it didn't just happen to me in Uniontown, Alabama.

It happened to other people, I'm sure, that got involved—that was left, marched . . . whatever. But in Uniontown, Alabama, it wasn't but six of us that got involved, and not one of the six quite naturally, went to college, not a single one. Not a single one. No, not a single one. Well, my brother—now I went after I went to the military—you know—and got my GI bill, and I came back and I used my GI bill to pull myself up by my bootstraps. But to go out of high school into college—'cause my brother graduated and after he got to be a grown man, went to Detroit and came back, oh, you know, way after the years. Went to Severn University—I went to Severn University—started at Severn University. My brother started off at Severn University after he went to Detroit and worked in the factories, came back, went to Severn University then after that went on to A&M University. And went on with John Morris. But to go out of high school, like everybody else, that didn't happen to me 'cause we was the only two. My brother and I was the only two at that went to college at all. The other three just, you know, faded off into the sunset. [Laughter]

Did your father experience any repercussions?

No, my daddy was a permanent Baptist preacher known for his message, so he didn't have a problem. He was pastoring in Selma and he was a renowned hoopalistic preacher that everybody liked to hear speak, so Daddy didn't have any problem with that at all. I mean, they expected that of him. It was a situation where, you know, "That's Rev. Flowers . . ." That's him anyway, so it wasn't a big deal. Daddy was not a part of the college-graduating ministers, so he didn't have to worry with that esteem on his back.

Is your business there [in Uniontown] too?

Oh yeah, but only different now. The same people who was probably there when I was in high school who was over the churches—and I'm now the chair of the deacon board and—oh my God—for his leadership. I guess the thing is, the cream get to the top! And here I am. You know? And everything that was done to hold me back have failed. And I guess if there's any such thing as cream of the crop, that's me! You know, I'm not boasting, but far as wealth or anything else that goes along with that part of life . . . you know, that's me.

I'm an RV owner and a Mercedes Benz owner and a Lexus owner and the whole nine yards. Property and everything else that goes along with success, if you ask me about such things in that ballpark. So the move for me to fail just fell altogether. 'Course God was on my side from day one without a shadow of a doubt. I wouldn't be where I am without God—just was a part of the history.

But, now let me go ahead just—then I'll let you finish. Even with that—Mr. Turner and all that happened back then, I moved. I went on to become chairman of this county. Mr. Turner and I ended up working side by side, and he ended up working to support me as chairman, and he worked under me. I became chairman and he became vice-chair—[of the] Perry County Commission.

I stayed chairman for this county eighteen years. And so Mr. Turner became vice-chair under me and he and I ended up working side-by-side for many years 'til he died, so that kinda give you the real history. After we went through all that, and I go off to the military, he's still here—I came back. I run for county commissioner some many years later and I win. And then Mr. Turner and I end up sharing the same commission together.

Alright, so I'm familiar with some of the political gains that were made in Marion right after the march, into the seventies and into the late seventies—the election of certain officials—black public officials. Was that kind of thing happening in Uniontown at the same time?

Andrew Hayden, the political thing, became like Albert Turner became known in the Marion area. But Andrew Hayden also became the first black councilman in Uniontown, Alabama. He became the first black mayor of Uniontown, Alabama. So you see where I'm going. Albert Turner got involved up here and then Andrew Hayden still maintained. . . .

And when was that? When did he become the first black mayor?

During that first era of the seventies. He probably became the first councilman during the seventies . . . and then he became the mayor somewhere in that neighborhood. Eighties, early eighties [or] seventies. Well, in the seventies he probably became mayor.

When was the bridge created between Uniontown and Marion?

When Johnny Flowers became chairman of Perry County Commission. 'Cause I was living in Uniontown, Alabama. Now you have the divide which was between Albert Turner and Hayden, and Johnny Flowers was a young kid that came from Uniontown, was part of the Marion thing—which I was never respected for it in the Uniontown area—but now all of a sudden, I got to be the [inaudible] enough so now I became chair of the county.

How did you come to do that? What kind of obstacles did you have to overcome to become chairman?

Well, my construction business was successful, so that part was already kind of—and so my name was well-known. And then Andrew Hayden at this point is, this is Uniontown and he successful and this sort of stuff, so he was chairman of the ADC, Mayor Hayden was, of Uniontown, Perry County, and DC—and Mr. Turner was chairman of new South up here—I got endorsed by ADC.

What's ADC?

Alabama Democratic Caucus. Political group. So, Mayor Hayden endorsed me in the Uniontown area because Mr. Turner was against me.

Johnny Flowers

So, it's like Uniontown gotta beat Marion—sure. We gotta do it with Johnny Flowers and [inaudible words] I was delivered at that time by the Alabama Democratic Caucus, along with all of the white vote in Perry County. I got all of the white vote, along with the other people who wasn't controlled by Mr. Turner. I'll leave it like that.

I was self-employed and I had my own business, so I was a different breed—you see, I was a different person—from the perspective of the white side—because I was a businessman. And what happened back then—even now, really—they usually try to pick up educated blacks, course I came up disappointing to them, but usually you end up getting an educated black and then that educated black who owns something will forget the other blacks eventually. You get my point. And you might say I was seen as somebody of that nature, because here's someone who already have, so we don't have to worry about him trying to get—and so he already think that he more so he's not gon' worry about these folks down there. We're just gonna pick him up. Well they did—they voted for me. At the same time, Mr. Turner had the same attitude about me, "Johnny Flowers is, oh, white . . ." Whatever—so he fought me tooth and nail . . . and he wanted to become county commissioner and he ran on that, and he ran a person against me in that race to make sure that I'd lose, cause Mr. Turner wanted to be chair, and after all old Johnny Flowers is an old white Uncle Tom.

So, now, I got all of Uniontown, and all the white votes, and Mr. Turner against me—never ran for politics ever in my life. Had no idea how I ran what I ran—I was at home watching the Braves baseball game.

And we had just went through a court order, and my wife came in and said, "They got a meeting at St. Hall [inaudible]—you going?" I said, "Aw, I'm going to support Essex," was who Mr. Turner wanted in the first place. And they threw out their election so they got to re-vote again. I said I'm going to support Essex! And my wife said, "Well I'm going to go to St. Hall and see what's going on—I've got the kids here and all." Aaah, okay. I'll go with Al and they say, "When are they gonna come through and talk to us about what's going on with the election [when I got there]." Oh, Mr. Flowers, they already gonna come through and talk to us. . . . What do you mean they're not gonna talk to us? And I said, well, you all need somebody to represent you. I'll do it. That's how I ended up running in the first place. And they said, well, about four of us got in the race, and of course not one, but at that point Mr. Turner says, "Johnny Flowers, Uncle Tom, we don't want Johnny Flowers," and blah, blah, blah. And so then, we end up with this divide.

I won. Mr. Turner had two hundred absentee ballots before I even got started. Never ran before, but I got in the runoff. Me and Essex. Then Mr. Turner says, "You might as well go home. I have three hundred absentees, and the runoff, and you never ran before, and you have to get three hundred people to come to the poll just to get it even with me." And I said, "Yeah, but I think I'm gonna get you—I'm gonna beat ya." I went out and got a deputy registrar. I had never seen an absentee ballot in my life. I didn't even know what one looked like. I went out and got a deputy registrar. And because the white community was on my side I can get anything I want as far as that's concerned. So anyway, I got a deputy registrar who could register people on Saturday night while they was out partying, and then I somehow or another ended up with fifty absentees that I'd never ever seen before in my life. Everybody that voted for me the first time around. I went back to them and said, "Can I count on you?" 'Cause I was the organizer, and of course they says, "Yeah, well we gonna be looking at your name." I told 'em, "Well, if you're not at the polls, I'm gonna come and see about you!" And he said, "Can I come and see about you if you're not here by five?" He'd do it. I had everybody came back and voted for me and I won by fifty votes in the runoff.

Now the power struggle happened that I wasn't even—that I didn't even want. Mr. Turner wanted to be the chair. I didn't

Johnny Flowers

run for the county commissioner to be chair. I wanted to run for county commission just to be an old commissioner. But now that I won and I had to struggle with Mr. Turner, surely I'm not gonna vote to make him chairman!

So now, the lot fell upon me. And there was two white commissions and three blacks. . . . And I wasn't gonna vote to make Mr. Turner chairman. I wasn't gonna vote to make one of the white boys chairman. So the two white boys gonna vote to make me chair, along with me!

So, now I'm chairman. But little did I know that the county was bankrupt—they didn't have a quarter. And everybody walked out of the office and quit. All the clerks, all the engineers, everybody. But I wasn't what Mr. Turner thought I was—a fighter against him. And a fighter against what he stood for, far as integration, far as freedom of black people in Perry County, I wasn't against what he stood for. In fact there wasn't ten cents difference between me and Albert Turner. It's just that the people said that. They didn't know I marched all the way. They didn't know my feet was blistered. And Mr. Turner knew I had marched all the way. And he knew I had fought to march all the way, with Charles White—even when he had wanted to kick me out of the line. But at the same time because I had the white support, and had the side of politics on my side, he assumed that I was fighting against him.

And so he wanted Walter McKinnon to be the clerk for commission after everybody had quit. And I went to Mr. McKinnon and says, "I'm not going to not hire you because Mr. Turner wants you hired." I said, "If you can do this job, it's yours." So that was my first melting pot right there. So I hired Mr. McKinnon when Mr. Turner—they said, "Well, he's Mr. Turner's choice," so what? If he can do the job! I came on as chair, and I brought him aboard.

And then Mr. Turner fought me the first two years, and I won again 'cause I drew the short straw, because the judge had ruled that everybody that run had to run and get new people. So, and all five commissioners ran at once, so two of us ran over a two-year period, had to run again two more years afterward—that was me and the other commissioner. So, Mr. Turner, I never had to quit running 'cause I was running again two more years, and Mr. Turner kept running against me 'cause he still wanted to be chair! I still won. Two years later I won again, but then, I eventually moved that old myth between Mr. Turner and I. He finally realized that Johnny Flowers is not all that bad. . . .

How did you mend the divide?

Well, I guess I'll start off with Mr. McKinnon—and then I didn't have no problem with other people Mr. Turner wanted to get hired. I didn't fight it. You know, and we had our biggest showdown—quite naturally I had this white vote that I owed and Hank Sanders was the attorney. The county attorney Hank said to me, "You're gonna have to pay these white people sooner or later." I'll deal with that when the time comes! I'll deal with it. It wasn't that I wasn't trying to pay the white people. I'm pretty good in doing whatever I need to do. Mr. Turner, wife Evelyn—we're the best of friends to this day. A spot came open in the voter's registrar's office, and I was chairman of the county. Turner was in that office as far as being hired. And I says, "Mr. Turner you could have at least asked me, you know, at least. You want her to be in your office." He said to me, "I didn't need you to tell me. I don't need to get your permission."

"But at least you could have respected me as chairman!" I didn't need that. Then I said to him, you know, I realize there was a time when I'm gonna have to shoot my gun as chairman of this county, and I says, I'm gonna have to shoot it now. He say, "Ain't nothing you can do about it. You understand?" Stan was the state senator, Jenkins Brown was the state representative. They had got this done behind my back. And Hank Sanders's word to me was, "It's done." Nothing you can do about it. All the white folk was calling and they were saying, "Johnny

Johnny Flowers

Flowers, you should move out of this office—I mean, she gotta go, man." I said, well, I guess it's time for me to shoot my chairmanship gun. So I told Mr. Turner, I'm gonna have to move your wife out of the voter registrar's office. Hank Sanders say, "You can't do it no way. Hank Sanders is senator, Jenkins Brown's the representative. You can't move her!" I said, "We'll see."

Well, all the telephone calls, and finally, you know what happened. She got moved.

And around what year was this?

Oh, it's kind of hard for me to say. It was during my fourth . . . I had won my first two years and I got elected my second term, so it was a four-year term. So it was during that. I was elected in '88, so it was around maybe '92, somewhere in that ballpark—around '92 or '93. And I went over there. I had the governor and he says, well you know I'll sign if you get the Ag man to sign, and you know the Ag man didn't want to sign because he said he was going to cut me out of his budget and all this sort of stuff. But all these people was calling—all the white folk was calling—and I was going over there every day and saying, "Man, you gotta move her." Eventually, I won.

And then, when this happened—when this happened—quite naturally, Mr. Turner, along with Senator Sanders, and along with Jenkins Brown, realized finally that Johnny Flowers has got to be one monster. You understand me. It really was. Because here you had Hank Sanders, a senator, and he had got this done for Albert, and now I've gotten it undone. . . . Boy this is something! So now all these white folks—he done teamed up with these white folks? He's a monster! But that wasn't me! So now, I said, we need to have a meeting. So we did. Hank Sanders, Albert Turner, Robert Turner, John McAlpine . . . yes . . . John McAlpine—he and I was friends at that time. John McAlpine, Turner, Robert Turner, Albert Turner, and Hank Sanders. We met in Robert Turner's office. His brother.

I have a brother—baby brother. Robert and I always got along. And so, and I told Robert, I want you to chair this meeting. When Robert got in the room, he says, "What do you all want from Johnny Flowers? Albert? He's given you everything you want. He hired Mayor Atkins, he hired Ward—what do you want? And the man is chairman you won't even think enough of him . . . you're just running over him!"

And of course we sit in the room and I says, "I'm not in this room to grease the track, 'cause I know what you all want me here." I said, "I'm going to stand my grounds because I want respect." I said, "You don't have to like me or love me, but I want to be respected as chair if I'm the chairman. I don't want to be run over by no one—even you, Senator." They understood.

And then Robert Turner, who was chairing, he says, "It's time for you all to let it be, you know. Leave it alone! Let's end this craziness!" And then, so Albert say, "Okay, it's over." And we walked out of that room with a brand-new attitude and a whole new perspective, and the county got busy. I stayed chairman, even though every election, that commission would elect a new chair. It wouldn't automatically—I wouldn't be elected by the people. Each commission, every time we'd have an election, every two years, we'd have a new rotation and that commission could elect anybody they want to be chairman. I mean, I was just sitting there. And every year after that I would be re-elected to serve as chair. And I stayed there for eighteen years. I went in there and got elected, and then they made me chair when I got elected, and then I stayed chairman until I left!

Do you think in the long run that was a more powerful position to hold?

To this day, because of the perspective I brought to the chair, you know, I didn't just serve. I probably never had a vote without a white vote while I was chair. Wouldn't have raised a thing. I might have had maybe two or three votes on a landfill project that the white commission wouldn't have voted "maybe," but all other times I've always had a white vote. Wasn't like it is now. Now it's almost black and white. I served as chairman, I served as the chair. I also kept a black person—a white and black employee in the commissioner's office when I was chair. Walter Meade was the chief clerk but always I told them we're the majority, and the majority always have the minority. And I told them that. So, they understood. And I would try to keep that. I always tried to keep a white person under Ms. Kenny in that office. And I got it where the white person didn't want to be under her—they wanted it to be top notch.

And if they couldn't be at the top, they didn't want to serve. And eventually, after maybe about twelve years, I think maybe more—fourteen years, I think—I kept it that way for about fourteen years. I stayed there eighteen. I think the last four years I was there it was all-black in office, but I think up until then it was a black and white office.

Whatever happened with Hayden?

Andrew Hayden. No, he served as mayor until Jenkins Brown. I mentioned Jenkins Brown was the state representative. Jenkins Brown, but now prior to Hayden, he was mayor. Probate judge at that time and Hayden was real good buddies—and it was kind of like a deal between the two of them that the white probate judge says, when I no longer want the job, I'll support you for the job, told Hayden. They was good political buddies.

Support him for the mayorship, or...

No, for the probate judge job . . . See Hayden was mayor of Uniontown, and the probate judge job—He was white and he was on the same political thing . . . they was like, buddy-buddies . . . and the probate judge says, "When I no longer want to be probate judge, I'll support you for being probate judge—it was kind of like a deal. So finally this probate judge just decided that he didn't want to run again. That's when I ran for county commission. And I became the first chair, 'cause until then, the probate judge was the chair of the county commissioner. I became the first county commissioner chair of Perry County. Until then it was the probate judge. So, Hayden ran for county commissioner. So, Hayden ran for probate judge when I ran for county commissioner. But now the law is that I was going to be the chair, because the law had passed. So the old judge was like, I'm not gonna serve as probate judge if I'm not gonna chair the commission. So a new day was in the horizon. So Hayden ran for probate judge. It was kinda like an agreement that you would support me, but then this probate judge supported his son! His son ran for probate judge. And, [the] Albert Turner—machine—backed that white probate judge's son over Andrew Hayden.

Why?

Ah—just because—political enemies all these years and we're not going to support Andrew Hayden because they "free" down there and his views are not our views and we won't be caught dead. I'd rather vote for this white guy than to vote for him. [Laughter]

How is it that you think Albert Turner came to realize that you were on the same side?

The love for the county kind of surfaced. My love for the county and Albert Turner love for the county surfaced. Albert Turner learned that Johnny Flowers loved the county just like I loved the county. And when I started pushing for jobs, and that's what Albert Turner wanted, when I started pushing for courthouses being closed at 12 o'clock, I didn't want it closed, he didn't want it closed. When we started pushing for, you know, just basically the same things.

Same agenda.

Same agenda. 'Cause our goal was the same! And once he realized that, and then I got involved with community development, and I got involved with economic development, right? Wanted to bring home a little landfill and jobs, and Albert Turner saw that he wanted the same thing. Then the white community said, "We don't want this! We don't want this prison. We don't want this landfill." And then I needed Mr. Turner's support—the idea that we need these jobs! We need this landfill project and we need the prison—you're talking about two hundred jobs.

So, at this point, the white community starts standing up in court, saying, "If you're going to continue to move in the direction that you're moving in, we're not gonna support you. We're gonna vote you out next election. We're gonna vote you out next election. This is the white community. And they knew they could, 'cause they were expecting Mr. Turner to continue. Mr. Turner ran somebody against me for two years in a row because he wanted that chair seat. So for two years, he ran somebody against me. But now, this white man says, "We don't like your agenda, Mr. Flowers, and we're gonna vote you out. We're not gonna support you next time."

The white community says, "We don't like what you're doing! We tell you we don't want the landfill, we tell you we don't want a prison, and you're determined to move in this direction. We're gonna vote you out. We're not gonna be supporting you next time around." And they came to commissioner board, stood and pointed their finger—"You are gone!"

So at this point, Mr. Turner's group, when my election time came around, and Mr. Turner met with his crowd, and they still was like, someone going against Johnny Flowers. I mean, you can't—and Mr. Turner says, "Well, we not gonna have the white folks telling a person when he's gonna stay in office and when he not gonna stay in office, so we're gonna support Johnny Flowers." And they were like "uh . . ." and he says, "Yeah, but, we ain't gonna have the white folks tellin' people when they gonna stay in and when they gonna get out, and at this time, Mr. Turner knew that our agenda was the same, so, they supported me, instead of against me. So, I won. Now, you know, without a shadow of a doubt, quite naturally if I was winning without Mr. Turner, surely, with him I was just a landslide. So now all of a sudden, that's what ended the whole thing. We ended up with one county at that point.

And so at that point, how significant was the white vote? What were the demographics like at that time?

Well, and it's still now! I'm sitting here now talking to you out of that seat because of that white vote. It's 65/35, somewhere in that ballpark.

But now I wasn't at-large [inaudible]. I'm in a district so my district still was like 65 percent black and 35 white. But having all of that 35 percent white vote give that district an edge if that 35 percent is on your side. And the difference between the white vote and the black vote—if the white vote commit you got that 35 percent—totally. It's not like the black vote—they'll talk about it but you don't really have it. But they—once they give it, they gives it!

And I lost a seat because of the same reason I won the seat. I wouldn't give up on things that I wanted done—the agenda. And they says, "We against that agenda and we don't want you to have it," and then, by this time they had got enough black people to go along with that idea that "you don't need this, you don't need that—he's pushing towards this, he's pushing towards that—and you all don't need this and you don't need that." And so now you got enough black folks in my district says, "These white folks are right!" Quite naturally I lost the seat at that point, which was time. You know, I was ready to go anyway. I achieved permission.

So that's how I ended up losing the seat. I lost it when the white vote got to the black vote and said, "You all need to vote against him at this point."

And there ain't not but ten cents between me and Turner. . . . So now the old man was dead and little Albert, and they said to me, "You never voted out of all these years not one vote against the Turners." Never. Not one vote. I says, "Well, yeah, you right! I don't know whether it's the Turners—I've never voted against wrong. If it was right, it was right! I never voted against wrong!"

And where old man Albert and young Albert was more vocal—they was outspoken and calling them the snakes, they ended up calling me one because I was very quiet and never let go. I still tell little Albert this now: My granddaddy used to say, if you let people know where you coming from they'll block your pathway. With me, they never knew where I was coming from 'cause I never spoke out. I was going to all their meetings and go to all their funerals, and go to all their businesses. You know, I mean, I was chairman of the county. I would go to their houses and drink coffee. You know, I was chairman of the county, but I wasn't a racist far as out-front talking.

So, what are you doing these days?

When I was with the commissions, I served as president of the Association of County Commissions, State of Alabama. Whole bunch, from Mobile to Birmingham—now I'm with Resource Conservation Development (RC&D), I was the first black president of the state of Alabama for that; I'm on the national board of resource conservation in Washington, DC. It's an eighteen-member board throughout the whole United States of America, from Hawaii to Alaska, and I am the only African-American on that board in Washington, DC. I have a budget of 50.7—fifty-million point seven-hundred thousand. I'm the only African-American on that board. So I'm still part of that, and I'm president of that. My local council Resource Conservation

Development—'course, given that the little grants here and there, it's what I do. And still doing my construction business. I build churches for a living. Haven't missed a day off of one—probably twenty-five years.

Wow—that's quite a story. Anything else that you think you might be forgetting, that you think you want to—

Well, that's basically it. But I gotta say this—I'm an old Baptist preacher's son. And if it wasn't for my religion and my faith in God, none of it would have took place. I turned sixty years old when I was in Albuquerque, New Mexico, and they called me up this group RC&D. I think it was about four, five thousand people there for the meeting and they got ready to start it. And they called upon me to do the prayer, 'cause I'm known for the prayer.

Even when I was county commissioner chair over the state of Alabama—president—I was known as the praying commissioner. I was the first one ever to brought prayer to the meetings—so I'm known as the praying person. Out there on my sixtieth birthday, he said, "We're gonna ask our national board member Johnny Flowers to come up and pray—open us up—and then when I was on my way up, my mom, she says, "And by the way, today is Johnny's birthday," and can you imagine a roar of "happy birthday" from a crowd that size? [laughter] If you ask me what I contributed, truly it would be my faith in God, would be the bottom line. I prayed my way to the top. No ifs, ands, buts. It wouldn't be no other way.

Now I don't know where we're headed to, far as economics. I just can't see what the future is with us in the long haul. And by the way, a judge ran for the state representative and all the counties involved voted for me except for my county. I lost my county. If I won my county, I would've been the state representative. My people in Perry County, they voted against what I had done. They wasn't voting about what I could do. They knew I could do it. They voted against, more or less, based upon what he have already done. And that was a very interesting concept of a voting.

I lost about fifteen hundred votes. And I lost because his county voted for him fifteen hundred more than my county voted for me. My county voted for him more than they voted for me. I think I lost Perry County on the votes. And then his county carried him fifteen hundred votes over me. Same difference. But I won all of the outside counties. But I couldn't carry my own!

The beautiful part of that whole part of politics—I sing at my church, I'm a deacon at my church, and I sing in the choir, I'm a soloist and all that. I had people in my choir sing behind my leadership as a leader of the choir—didn't vote for me, didn't support me. Politics is a very, very tough thing. Especially when you're getting the job done. If I had just went in office and did nothing, I'd have been there right now. Could've stayed there for life. However, I did something. I created a vacuum of people screaming and yelling and hollering. And it's more about, you do what we want you to do, and you'd be surprised and I don't know how religious you are, but you'd be surprised the people who has come to politics. They don't want you to do what God wants you to do. [They say] God ain't got nothing to do with this [laughter]. You out your mind! This not a God thing! We don't want you to do it! And with me, I'm a faster and prayer and all that sort of thing. And I says, it's not about me and if the Lord and my prayer wasn't about, "Lord, me." If I'm doing something that you don't want me to do, don't let it happen. But if it's your will, then let me be that instrument to get it done.

And I stood alone—I mean, alone. And the people from ABM said, "Man . . . ," and they got all the people pointing their fingers: "You crook! You thief!" And all this—"You took all this money from these landfill folks!" And I paid money out of my own pocket to travel and go and spend nights. And I sit there and we went through all that process. And then when it was over, then the guy says . . . "Okay, what they say if you dot every 'i' and cross every 't' you're gonna get your permit." That's why I'm gonna make sure all my 'i's and 't's are dotted. And that's what happened. And when I was on my way out of office, they was on their way in with the jobs and the whole nine yards. Politics, to me, if you don't love people, it has nothing to do with you. If you don't want to be that sacrificial lamb, then don't get involved, 'cause it has nothing to do with the smiling and grinning. Smile in your face, they'll pat you on the back, but when it gets to the political realm of it all, they would, like I told some of the people at my church who supported me, and I had a lot of them who did not, and I says—"My church family and those of you in this church who supported me. . . . I realize that there were a lot of sheep—goats with sheep clothes on." And I says, "And I understand that in the end only God separates the goats from the sheep." No, so you see I don't have no problem with that. I understand that we all are different. And it went down that way. You know. And it turned out well. Cost me about twenty-five grand to run, you know [laughter]. But I was able to do it. And what happened in the future, that sad part about it—what happens when you have someone who is unable to do it? And even though I didn't win, but I gave the people a good choice. I was out-manned by the white community after. With all the people with the campaign donations who campaigned for my appointment. They didn't want me because I was independent. I wasn't strong enough to run. They couldn't silence me. They couldn't speak for me.

So, if you had to, in a sentence or a phrase, capture the essence of your career and life and what was essential about your experience growing up, experiencing the march, watching all the changes that had taken place in this county up until this point, what would you say?

Change, change, change, change. I think I was talking to the young people the other day about it. I came up in an era and a time when the "n-word" was on the lips of just about every white person. And I came up when you had to go through the back-door just to get your ice cream cone. And I came up when, even when you was going to the back door to get that ice cream cone, they talked about the Auburn-Alabama game and you stayed there and waited 'bout fifteen minutes until finally they turned and said, "Boy, what kinda ice cream cone you want!" And you better not walk away from that window—the idea of talking about, "I'm tired of waiting." Because they'd went out there and beat you upside the head. I came out of that era, all the way up until where we are and I've seen houses that were lived in by those people, who are dead now, and black folks are living in the very same houses. When you put it all on paper, I see a generation of people who started off losing their lives to get the right to vote to a generation of people who get mad with you when you come to their house to ask them to vote. I've had that happen to me: "Get off my—Get away from me!"

That's the only time when I've cried—because I came from both corners where I was beat up for trying to get the right to vote, to the point where I been driven from the same people's steps. I've lived long enough to witness both sides of the coin. Can you imagine? [Laughs] Isn't that something? And I witnessed it. Back when we got our first black congressman, and I was going around to all of the white people that I knew and that knew my dad and knew my granddad, to get funds to help get this guy elected. And I was campaigning for a guy named Sam Taylor although he had won. But I was campaigning for Sam Taylor. And Sam was in the office working in Washington, DC, with, um, Clark Harrison. And the white people knew Sam because he would help with getting that paperwork through. So I was down here working with Sam Taylor and I built Sam Taylor dad's house, so I was working. And I was going around with these guys begging money for Sam and several white guys said to me, "Johnny Flowers, you know we gonna need money for Sam Taylor."

Do What the Spirit Says Do

But I'm gonna tell you. They said, "You black people got to learn to pay your own way!" Now that you're getting ready to get your own congressman, you want us to give you the money to—for him to run! Yeah, doc, this particular fellow is named "Dr. Weistime."

I said, "But yeah, Doc, until black folk learn how to tithe, you always gotta help us." "Yeah, you gotta pay your way . . . you gotta pay your own way!" But he said this—he said, "I'm gonna be dead in my grave, he said, but, when it first started, we should have let the educated blacks vote. We should've let those who own land voted. And the ones who had a job. So, these [inaudible] little votes wouldn't hurt us at all. He said, "Yes, but the right to vote was so important to us—we didn't want to hardly have not even one!" He said, "We made a mistake. We shouldn't have done that . . . ," he said, "because they didn't want you to have a single vote. Now all of the welfare folks and everybody vote . . . ," he said, "we messed up . . ." He said, "Don't worry." He said, "I'm gonna be dead in my grave. . . ." He said, "It's your cabinet but we're gonna get it back. . . ." He said, "Black people is very lazy, you see, and they're very complacent, and they're gonna stop voting." He said, "We're gonna get it back." He said, "When we get it back, we're gonna know what to do with it next time." He said, "Sure I'm gonna be dead . . . ," he said, "but it's gonna happen."

Well, what happened the other day when the vote went down and we lost in Alabama—didn't but fifty-seven people out of a hundred voted, and we lost, and the state of Alabama went all Republican. And I thought about what he said when black people and them went to the houses to ask them to vote and they was running me off their porch, and the tears running down my cheek. And I told Doc what I was seeing at that time. I said, "Doc, the only thing about what you said to me, that I can't do—I can't call you a lie." And he laughed, 'cause he knew I couldn't. Now you ask me, what's gonna happen to people in Alabama—people in Perry County, Alabama, even? We are not conscientious to the point where we understand the importance of the whole process. Yeah, we fought for the right to vote because we didn't have it—'cause that's how we are when you got something that I can't have. Forget about *want*. If you tell me I can't have it, my goodness! You just done made me mad! But then when I get where I can get it, and have it, then it's just like, I don't really like it anymore. It's not worth anything. I got it, and, "So what?"

And that's what has happened to us as a race of people with this community. We have it, and the value of having it just don't have a value anymore. And because of that, we're gonna lose.

Do you think it's the same people who once understood the value of it that no longer have it, or do you think it's the younger generation?

I think it's the people who of my age—people who don't speak to their children. The children have no idea how they received it, nor the value of it, because they have not been taught the struggle of it all. Oh sure, there's Dr. Martin Luther King and the whole nine yards, and I shared this with my Sunday school class the other Sunday morning. And they, for the first time only because they was in my class, understood. And I said to them, "Do you know why Dr. Martin Luther King's name is on more streets and more roads and more boulevards in history? Do you all know why?" . . . Um, no, Mr. Flowers. I said, "You all don't wanna take a crack at it? Do you wanna know why?"

Well, it started off with one McDonald's where black folks couldn't go to. And all of a sudden, they was integrated. And not only that they was integrated, see, black people in America spending-wise, is the third-largest country in the world. We don't save any money. We spends it. And because we are economical boon and spends all we get, and because we was segregated, and they was keeping our little money, and the white man standing up there, he wouldn't give me the ice cream cone. But once we boycotted, and wouldn't nobody go in there and he couldn't pay his house note, he's talking about Auburn football game and Alabama until he couldn't pay his housenote—and once the black people boycotted and stopped spending—period—you know they couldn't pay any notes.

Then all of a sudden they stopped this, and all of a sudden this "yessir" and "yes ma'am" started comin' from the old white down to the little children, because I gotta pay my house note. Well, Dr. Martin Luther King now only had one McDonald's because of interracial and black folks started spending money. When they opened up the doors, we started spending and now we have one McDonald's and we put a McDonald's on every corner. We put a Burger King everywhere. And we put businesses everywhere that there's a business need to be—because black folks . . . spends money. And because of that, the economical side of this country realized, if it was not for Martin Luther King . . . if it was not for Martin Luther King, we wouldn't have all of these businesses. All of the JC Penney's, all of the K-Marts and—'cause black folks spend money! [Laughter] And we thank this man for the bottom of our hearts! And the least we could do for him, the least we could do—I'm talking about the whites in the community—the least we could do is name these streets and boulevards.

I mean, it's the least we could do, 'cause if it wasn't for him—if it wasn't for Martin Luther King and his marching and all of the things that he done to bring the black folks, and sit him into our restaurants, he made us one rich group of people.

That's it. But even with that, our people don't understand that without the vote, we lose it all. And we, our children, are satisfied with the McDonald's and the hamburgers and all the places. They do not understand economically we still are the highest unemployed people in the country.

Ain't that something? Ain't that something? Amazing. Truly amazing.

Well, that's it—that's the Johnny Flowers story of it all.